Sexual Abuse Recovery *by His Spirit*

Emily Getzfreid

For Virginia,

whose courage, strength,

and pertinacity inspired every word.

Come Forth, Beloved

Out of your darkness
Out of your shame
Out of your past that
Holds you like chains
Out of your wounds
Out of your pain

Out of the shroud that wraps you in blame
Come out. Come forth. Come in, Beloved.

Into the light
Into the rain
Into blood
That cleanses
Every stain
To blessing
To freedom
To love unchanged
That heals
That provides
That ever remains.

Sexual Abuse Recovery By His Spirit was written to be used in conjunction with a HOPE FOR HER sexual abuse recovery group. More information about HOPE FOR HER can be found at HopeforHERMinistries.com. There you will find information about groups in your area, as well as all the resources you need to host a sexual abuse recovery group in your home church. The leaders at HOPE FOR HER Ministries want to connect with you, so please reach out to them through the website or the HOPE FOR HER Facebook page.

HOPE FOR **HER MINISTRIES**

HOPE FOR HER *is a sexual abuse recovery ministry whose mission it is to provide female sexual abuse survivors a safe opportunity to pursue emotional healing, experience encouragement through God-centered community, and rest in the promise of God's faithful presence: for the Lord her God will be with her wherever she goes.*

The purpose of HOPE FOR HER is simple: to provide sexual abuse survivors with hope for healing, encouragement, and rest. We believe the promise in scripture that the Lord is able to do immeasurably more in us than we could ever ask for or imagine by His Spirit[1], and with that in mind, we believe we have no reason to settle for just being "better"— better than we used to be, more healed than we were. We no longer have to cling to the coping strategies we've developed over the years or continue striving to merely survive under our own power. Instead we can embrace a deeper trust, a new dependence on the One is who is ever faithful to prosper His children in His time and in His way. We can courageously press on in our journey to complete healing from the trauma and wounds of our sexual abuse experience.

However, many sexual abuse survivors don't feel courageous in their pursuit of healing, but are instead afraid to believe— to hope for freedom, to desire wholeness— because they can't imagine what healing might look like or how it might be attained. Brokenness we understand. But wholeness? Complete healing? We don't dare hope it's possible. That's why we need the encouragement that comes from a God-centered, truth-focused community. Scripture tells us that Christ is the head, and we are

---

[1] Ephesians 3:20

His body, each part supplying strength to the others[2]. Our faith, stories, testimonies, and breakthroughs are not for ourselves alone, but are also to be God's divine provision of encouragement and comfort to others with whom we are connected[3]. In the same way, our brokenness— our struggles, our fears, our wounds— is not to be carried alone[4]. In His goodness and grace, our Heavenly Father has provided us with community, a spiritual pipeline through which courage and comfort is poured into our hearts and then through us into the hearts of others, so that every need is met[5].

From community we draw the strength and courage to press on— to hope and to heal, but also to rest. Psalm 46:10 exhorts us, "Be still and know that I am God". Exodus 14:14 tells us, "The Lord will fight for you; you need only to be still." Yet stillness and rest are not our go-to responses to heartache (or anything else, for that matter). Spiritual rest is a discipline, a learned response, that comes from spending time with the Lord, learning who He is and who we are in Him. Rest is trust in action: trust that He is strong enough to keep us close when our emotions make us feel distant, powerful enough to heal our deepest wounds yet loving enough to enjoy us right where we are, and faithful enough to keep working on us no matter how long it takes. Rest is a vital part of our healing journey because it requires us to stop forcing ourselves to be okay by our own power, and to allow Him— the one who is able to do immeasurably more than all we can ask or imagine— to make us more than okay: completely healed, entirely whole, perfectly secure in Him.

---

[2] Ephesians 4:15-16

[3] 2 Corinthians 3-4

[4] Galatians 6:2

[5] Acts 4:34

Contents

Chapter 1: Beginning the Journey

When my first sexual abuse recovery group began, long before the book you hold in your hands was even an idea, someone asked me what I thought would be the biggest obstacle for the group. My answer was immediate: our biggest obstacle would be prioritizing our healing. As wives, mothers, employees/bosses, friends, volunteers—as *women*—putting ourselves last on the list of to-dos is almost second nature. We don't often pursue something that is purely for us—though in this case at least, everyone in our lives will benefit indirectly. We don't want to inconvenience others by taking time for ourselves—to attend a group (just for ourselves), to read (just for ourselves), even to pray (just for ourselves). We'll do all those things and more to benefit others, but solely for ourselves?

Probably not, because we too often fail to see ourselves as *worth* it.

Yet in order to experience everything God has for you, you must believe not only that God has invited you into a season of healing, but also that it is worth the effort required to fully participate.

You are worth the time you will spend throughout the week reading this book, reflecting on the content, and praying over your own heart.

You are worth the inconvenience to your family for you to attend a weekly HOPE FOR HER group meeting.

You are worth the emotional upheaval you'll undoubtedly experience—and then inflict on your family to some degree—as you see this journey through.

You are worth it.

You might not *feel* as if you are worth it. Chances are, you've already started an argument against the idea in your mind, cataloging all the reasons you shouldn't even begin this healing journey. You don't have time, first of all. Your kids have sports and piano and dance lessons. The get-home-from-work-cook-dinner-run-out-the-door-again rush is already too much, so you can't add another weekly commitment. Besides, you're *fine*, right? Your triggers are manageable, you've learned to cope, and you are better today than you were five years ago. So, what's the point of dredging up the past?

But here's the thing: just because you feel something doesn't mean it's true.

You might feel like you're not worth the inconvenience.

You might feel like you're as healed as you're going to get.

You might even feel like the pain of your past is somehow what you deserve, or that it's selfish to hope for more freedom than you've already obtained—but none of those things is true.

So today I encourage you to purpose in your heart to receive everything God wants to do in your life in this season, no matter what it takes. Decide that you will do more than just show up to your group every week. Decide that you will position your heart *and continue positioning your heart* to receive healing from the Lord even when it's hard, uncomfortable, or seemingly overwhelming—because it will be all those things and more at times. Decide that you will follow Him wherever He leads you, no matter how vulnerable you must be along the way, and that you will spend whatever time is necessary asking, seeking, and knocking, as the scripture says:

> *Ask and it will be given to you; seek and you will find;*
> *knock and the door will be opened to you.*
> *For everyone who asks receives; the one who seeks finds,*
> *and to the one who knocks, the door will be opened.*

Matthew 7:7-8 NIV

Because it also says this:

Now to Him to who is able to do
immeasurably more than all we ask or imagine,
according to His power that is at work within us.

Ephesians 3:20 NIV

God has called you to this season because He wants to do incredible, even unbelievable things in your heart and life. He wants to remove your shame (even the shame you didn't know you had), displace your fears, and speak truth to the deception that keeps you bound to your abuse experience. Your HOPE FOR HER group and the material in this book are some of the tools He will use, but the actual healing will come by His Spirit—and only by His Spirit. Your role in the healing process is to position your heart to receive. He will do the rest.

Preparing for your HOPE FOR HER group

The decision to attend a sexual abuse recovery group is a hard one to make. As mentioned above, you probably have a million reasons why you shouldn't or can't. Some of those reasons might be practical—busy schedules and overloaded time-commitments—but others are likely fear-based: fear of exposure, fear of judgment, fear that you are too broken to actually be healed. Fear that once you open that door—the door you've perhaps kept locked and barricaded for years or decades—what's behind it will overwhelm you so badly you might never recover.

"Not by might, nor by power, but by My Spirit, says the Lord Almighty."

To those fears, and to the infinite number of fears not mentioned, I can say this with confidence:

You're not alone.

You're not alone in your fears. You're not alone in your struggles or in the ways you

3

hurt. Unfortunately, given the culture in which we live, even in the church, you may never have had the opportunity to talk to other people of similar experience. You may never have heard someone else share about their sexual abuse experience or the aftermath. You may never have heard someone talk about their healing journey. The culture of silence and shame regarding sexual abuse keeps all of us quiet and in the dark—blindly searching for a way out yet terrified of turning on the light.

Yet in your Hope for HER recovery group you will experience the extraordinary freedom that comes just from sitting around a table with other women who understand what you feel, who know what you mean even when you can't explain it, who will walk with you on the journey from surviving sexual abuse to overcoming it completely. Women who will both encourage you not to settle for being "just okay" and also extend to you the grace and love you need when you're not okay at all.

And just as importantly, you will get to do the same for them. You'll get to reassure women who feel afraid they're too broken to be healed. You'll get to extend love and grace to ladies who feel they don't deserve it and walk alongside sisters who need to know they're not alone.

Your Hope for HER recovery group is meant be a safe place for every member to pursue emotional healing, experience the courage that comes from divinely-designed, truth-centered community, and learn to rest in the faithfulness and love of our Heavenly Father. However, it is not enough to say the group is safe; it must *feel* safe to the women who attend. Felt safety will be what draws women back each week when the temptation to quit is loud and insistent, when they experience triggers and emotional upheaval that in the past they would have repressed or ignored, but now they know they have a place to be understood and not judged.

This kind of atmosphere is an anomaly for most of us. Many women have never experienced a truly safe group of ladies who do not gossip, judge, or compare themselves to each other—but it *is* possible. The following section explains what you can do to contribute to the critical atmosphere of safety felt within your group.

Safe Person Do's and Don'ts

A safe group is made up of safe people—people who honor, respect, and act with sincere love toward others. Read through this list prayerfully, asking the Lord to help you to be a safe person for the women in your group.

As a safe person, you will:

- Honor your sisters by keeping their stories and even their names confidential.

- Hear your sisters' feelings and experiences without judgment or doubt, and without questioning whether or not they are "overreacting."

- Accept them exactly where they are.

- Believe, and therefore act and speak, as though their feelings are true and valid.

- Extend grace, mercy, and love, even when you disagree.

As a safe person, you will not:

- Try to fix another person.

- Tell someone how they "should" feel, think, believe, etc.

- Try to be someone else's Holy Spirit.

- Say things that could wound, shame, or silence someone.

- Push someone to share more than they're able or ready to share.

As you are safe for others, determine also to become a safe person for yourself. Having a safe person and a safe community to whom you can express your most difficult feelings and experiences is vital for your growth and healing, but the person with the greatest influence over your heart is *you*. You must learn to be safe for yourself, to treat yourself with love, grace, and mercy. For example, as a safe person, you will hear your sisters' feelings without judgment, doubt, or wondering if they're overreacting, so determine to do the same for yourself. Accept yourself where you are, validate your own feelings, and extend grace and mercy to your own broken heart. Don't tell yourself how you "should" feel. Don't indulge in self-talk that shames or wounds your own soul.

You are not less deserving of felt safety than the other ladies in your community.

You are not less worthy of kindness, grace, and mercy than they are.

When the voice of your inner critic is loud and angry, come back to this page and remind yourself that your heart deserves safety, too.

Take a moment to write out a prayer telling the Lord of your desire to be a safe person. Ask Him to help you grow into being safe for others as well as yourself.

A Word About Comparison

We know from scripture that it is unwise to compare ourselves to others and determine our worth and value based on what we see[6], but that doesn't stop us from doing it. In fact, comparison—and the judgments it brings with it—often happen so quickly and instinctively that we don't realize what we've done. In the context of a sexual abuse recovery group, comparison can be especially damaging to our emotional growth. For example, in your group you might hear stories that are "worse" than yours and think, "I shouldn't even be struggling. What happened to me wasn't that bad." You may also be tempted to compare your response to your sexual abuse experience to others' responses. You might hear common threads in other peoples'

---

[6] 2 Corinthians 10:12

stories and believe something is wrong with you if you didn't respond to your experience in the same way, or if your response was more extreme than others'.

Those kinds of comparisons can prevent you from fully engaging in the healing process. They feed into the lie that says, "I'm the only one." *No one else is as messed up as me. No one else has done what I've done or felt what I've felt.* Be on guard against those kinds of thoughts. When they arise, reject them immediately. Practice saying out loud, "No, I reject that thought as a lie." Then submit the thought to the Lord in prayer and invite Him to speak truth to your heart.

Sexual Abuse Recovery by His Spirit Chapter Contents

Each chapter of this workbook includes a few common elements:

1. A meditation verse. These verses have been chosen specifically to underscore the biblical foundation of each week's topic. Romans 12:2 tells us that we are transformed by the renewing of our minds. On your journey to emotional healing you will encounter countless thoughts and mindsets that are based on false judgments against yourself and false ideas about who God is; meditating on scripture is one practical step you can take to renew your mind with the truth. The first page of each chapter is designed for you to write the week's verse 5 times (once a day for five days). The scriptures will mostly be presented in the *New International Version (NIV)*, but you should write the verse in whichever translation speaks to you the most. Writing it every day is a simple way to create a habit of meditation. Spend a few minutes meditating on the verse when you write it, asking the Lord to show you how it applies to you specifically.

2. A weekly prayer prompt. Much like the meditation verses, these prayer prompts are designed to keep your heart focused on the topic at hand in order to maximize the attention you give to the healing process. Pray through the weekly prompt every day.

3. Chapter text and closing prayer.

4. Discussion questions and additional prayer prompts for each chapter are located at the end of each chapter. If a specific lie that you've believed, memory, or belief comes up, or if the Holy Spirit speaks a truth to your heart, use the space provided to write it down. These thoughts will be a treasure to you someday when you look back on your healing journey and see how far you've come.

You are worth the effort your healing journey will require. You are worth the inconvenience your loved ones may experience as you pursue emotional healing. You are not alone in your fears, your struggles, or in the ways you hurt. Additionally, your HOPE FOR HER group is meant to be a safe place for each member. You can contribute to the felt safety of your group by following the Safe Person Do's and Don'ts outlined above. You can learn to be a safe place for yourself as well as for others.

. . . .

Lord, I ask you lead me as I begin this journey toward emotional healing. I thank You for calling me to it, for providing this opportunity, and for being with me every step of the way. I submit the next few weeks to You and pray Your will would be done here in my heart just as it is in heaven. I ask You to be my strength and my courage when my soul wants to give up or run away. Hold me close, I pray. **Amen.**

The following pages include the meditation verse, writing exercise, and prayer prompt for this chapter.

Chapter 1 Meditation Verse

For everyone who asks receives; the one who seeks finds,
and to the one who knocks, the door will be opened.

Matthew 7:8 NIV

Day 1

_____

_____

_____

Day 2

_____

_____

_____

Day 3

_____

_____

_____

Day 4

_____

_____

_____

Day 5

_____

_____

_____

Write out a list of everything you want God to do in your heart and life as you read through this material and attend your HOPE FOR HER recovery group. You may want to write two lists, one that is completely real and honest, and a second that includes only the items you're comfortable sharing with your group.

"I want to be completely healed from the pain in my heart of not being protected by my mother from the monsters she allowed into our home.

I want to be a good wife, secure enough to open up fully to my husband without feeling fear.

I want to learn how to stop mistaking sex for love.

I want to minister to others without fear, guilt, and shame stopping me."

~Stacy

_____

_____

_____

_____

_____

_____

_____

_____

_____

_____

_____

_____

_____

_____

_____

_____

_____

_____

_____

_____

_____

_____

_____

_____

_____

_____

_____

_____

_____

_____

_____

_____

_____

_____

_____

_____

_____

_____

_____

This week's prayer prompt: pray through your list daily, specifically asking the Lord to do in your heart the things you've written down.

Chapter 2 Meditation Verse

Now to Him who is able to do immeasurably more than all we ask or imagine, according to His power that is at work within us.

Ephesians 3:20 NIV

Day 1

_____

_____

_____

Day 2

_____

_____

_____

Day 3

_____

_____

_____

Day 4

_____

_____

_____

Day 5

_____

_____

_____

Chapter 2 Daily Prayer

Lord, during this season, I want you to do more in me than
I could ever ask or imagine. More healing, more freedom than
I could have ever dreamed possible by Your Spirit at work in me.

Write out anything you hear in your spirit or feel while you pray.

Day 1

_____

_____

_____

Day 2

_____

_____

_____

Day 3

_____

_____

_____

Day 4

_____

_____

_____

Day 5

_____

_____

_____

Chapter 2: Biblical Foundations for Emotional Healing

As we begin our journey of healing by His Spirit, it is imperative that we have a sound biblical foundation. So many of the beliefs we hold about God, ourselves, and our abuse experiences are contrary to biblical principles without us realizing it. However, the Bible must be our standard for faith, hope, and truth. It is the only way we can understand God's heart toward us, His will for us, and the promises He has made to us that will carry us through.

Most of these principles and verses will probably be familiar, so as you complete this chapter ask the Lord to help you to see and hear them with new eyes and a new understanding of how they apply specifically to your life.

Principle #1:
Complete emotional healing is possible.

Now to Him to who is able to do immeasurably more than all we ask or imagine, according to His power that is at work within us.

Ephesians 3:20 NIV

For most abuse survivors, imagining what emotional healing might look or feel like is impossible. We've carried our pain in secret, bandaging our wounds as best we could on our own, for years—even decades. Childhood abuse means those wounds are all we've ever known. It's hard to picture a life free of triggers, coping strategies, and defense mechanisms, or to imagine who we might be without them. In fact, the very idea that one day you won't have any of those things probably sounds fantastical and preposterous.

But it's not.

Think back to all the stories in scripture where Jesus healed the sick, blind, and lame. Never once did He only partially heal someone. He restored the blind man's sight completely. He restored the man's withered hand perfectly. And the woman who had been dealing with the issue of blood for 12 years, the one who had spent all she had in her pursuit of healing? The Bible tells us she was completely healed[7].

Why then do we expect our emotional healing to be only partial?

When it comes to overcoming the pain and trauma of sexual abuse, many of us have limited ideas about what that could mean. We easily believe that we can get *better* but find it much more difficult to imagine that we could be healed completely. Ephesians 3:20 is our promise that God will do so much more—immeasurably, exceedingly, abundantly more—in our hearts than we can ask or imagine. Let it be a reminder to pray and believe for *more* healing, *more* freedom, *more* wholeness than you have ever hoped for.

Principle #2:
Prayer is essential to emotional healing.

"Arise, cry out in the night, as the watches of the night begin;
pour out your heart like water in the presence of the Lord."

Lamentations 2:19 (NIV)

All healing, whether it's physical or emotional, is a byproduct of prayer. Throughout the Gospels, stories of miraculous healing all share one common element: request. Sometimes it's the sick person, sometimes it's a friend, but someone *always* asks. Sometimes they even go to great lengths to put themselves where Jesus is. They *position themselves* to receive healing from the Lord.

---

[7] Mark 8:22-25, Matthew 12:9-13, Mark 5:25-34

Like the recipients of healing in the Gospels, we can position ourselves to receive healing. We do that by reading books like this one, attending churches and recovery groups that focus on healing, and by spending time with others who are on the same journey. Still, that is just how we position our physical selves. We must also position our *hearts* to receive healing. As abuse survivors, we tend to live our lives with our hearts positioned to bear our pain—to hide, deny, or cope with it. So, in order to experience healing by His Spirit, we must be willing to change the position of our hearts, to open them up to receive from the Holy Spirit. Changing the position of our hearts begins with spending time communing with the Lord in prayer.

Communion is defined as **the sharing or exchanging of intimate thoughts and feelings**. When we commune with the Lord, we share our intimate thoughts and feelings with Him. Over time we begin to exchange our thoughts for His as revelation pours into our hearts. **Revelation begins with communication**. We pour out our hearts to Him, and He fills us with the truth, love, and healing we need.

The kind of prayer described in Lamentations 2:19 is not the kind of prayer most of us engage in on a regular basis. First of all, in this context at least, it is not prayer for *others*. It is prayer for you. Second, it delves deep beneath the surface. Lamentations 2:19 prayer is about opening our hearts to the Lord—our intimate thoughts, our deepest feelings. It holds nothing back from Him—hides nothing, denies nothing, avoids nothing. If your heart was a bucket filled to the brim with the murky water of your insecurities, fear, and struggle, this kind of prayer would be more than splashing a little off the top in the Lord's direction. It would be you, dumping it all out at His feet, and asking Him to fill you back up with rivers of living water.

One way to practice Lamentations 2:19 pray is through Confession and Invitation: confessing[8] your thoughts and feelings to the Lord and inviting Him to move in your heart. We'll address this in more detail in a later chapter, but here are some examples for you to follow as you begin this new manner of praying.

Example Prayer of Confession

Lord, here's what's in my heart today—my fear, my desire, my insecurity, everything:

[8] To confess in this context means to "recognize and verbally acknowledge."

Here is what I want to be free from:
Here is how I feel about what I'm walking through:

Example Prayer of Invitation

Lord, what do you want to say to me about this? What is the truth I need?

Principle #3:
Sexual abuse may affect every area of our lives, but in Christ we have the hope of restoration for them all.

"A thief comes only to steal and to kill and to destroy.
I have come so that they may have life and have it in abundance."

John 10:10 (HCSB)

The Bible is clear that we have an enemy in this world. His name is Satan, and his goal is to steal from us, kill whatever is good and alive in us, and ultimately wreak whatever destruction he can in our lives. Sexual abuse is the perfect way to do that because it can create lifelong consequences in every area of our lives.

Some of those areas are our sexuality, our sense of self, and our mental health. The following is brief discussion of each area.

<u>Our Sexuality</u>

Our sexuality is the most obvious area affected by sexual abuse. In fact, the most common consequence of childhood sexual abuse is sexual dysfunction, which is any difficulty associated with the process of sexual intimacy. Sexual dysfunction can range from extreme anxiety and an inability to engage in sexual intimacy to life-altering sexual addictions. It is important to honestly acknowledge the ways your abuse experience affected your sexuality, and also to understand that sexual dysfunction does not mean you are weak, broken, or a failure. Take a moment to pray a prayer of confession (recognition and verbal acknowledgment) and invitation over your sexuality. Acknowledge to the Lord the ways you recognize your sexuality has been affected and invite Him to move in that area of your life. Write out your prayer below.

Our Sense of Self

Sexual abuse fundamentally changes the way we see ourselves. It most often leads to low self-esteem, low self-worth, and a distorted self-image. Though we all probably have an accurate idea of what low self-esteem looks like, we may not always recognize it for what it is. More than that, we can easily accept the manifestations of low self-esteem as "just the way we are," without seeing it as something the Lord desires to heal. Below is a list of common "symptoms" of low self-esteem. Read it through slowly and prayerfully, asking the Lord to help you see the truthful answer to each question.

Symptoms of Low Self-Esteem:

Self-loathing: a constant or even occasional feeling of hatred, disappointment, or frustration directed at yourself—your identity, personality, etc.

> Do you subject yourself to anger, judgment, and expressed frustration that you wouldn't inflict on someone else? (This can be through your spoken words or in your non-verbalized self-talk.)

> Do you experience anger and frustration about who or what you are?

Perfectionism: having unreasonably high expectations of yourself in regard to performance of any kind, including how you handle your life circumstances.

Do you have a constant fear of failure or judgment from others?

Do you find it difficult to be fair to yourself when you don't meet your own expectations?

Worthlessness: a feeling that you have no real value, no good qualities, or are deserving of contempt.

Do you feel you have nothing of value to offer those around you, or that they would be better off without you around?

Do you fear others finding out who you really are?

Sensitivity to Criticism: all criticism, including well-intended advice, feels like a personal attack meant to shame or judge.

Are your feelings easily hurt by criticism or suggestions for improvement?

Does criticism feel like it confirms your worst fears about yourself?

Self-imposed Silence: you do not speak up to share your thoughts, feelings, or ideas, even when staying silent causes you unnecessary suffering.

Do you feel like your thoughts and feelings are unimportant?

Do you struggle to express your feelings or stand up for yourself in difficult situations?

People-Pleasing: a compulsive need to help, please, or support others without regard to your own well-being.

Do you feel the need to please others in order to attain or maintain their love, admiration, or respect?

Do you feel compelled to go out of your way to help others, even to your own detriment?

You will have the opportunity to pray over your answers in the discussion questions for this chapter.

Our Mental Health

Survivors of sexual abuse are more likely to suffer from every kind of mental illness including addiction, depression, and anxiety. They are also more likely to develop eating disorders, to engage in self-destructive behavior, and to suffer insomnia. As with sexual dysfunction, it's important to acknowledge the way your sexual abuse experience affected your mental health. If you struggle with "blaming all of your issues" on sexual abuse, or if you don't believe your sexual abuse experience is the root of any mental health issues you may have, that's okay. Simply read through the list, honestly answer the questions, and allow the Lord to sort out the details.

Have you experienced any of the following?

- Depression

- Anxiety

- Addiction

- Eating Disorder

- Self-destructive behavior

- Insomnia

- Other? Identify:

_____

_____

_____

Please note: this material is neither intended nor equipped to diagnose, assess, or treat mental illness. If you suffer from any of these or another mental health issue, please pursue help from a trained medical professional, including a licensed therapist. Do not allow shame or the stigma of therapy to prevent you from pursuing healing in every available avenue.

When I meditate on what John 10:10 means to me, I imagine my life as a globe of light. Every area that has been affected by my abuse experience is dark where it should be light, dead where it should be spiritually and emotionally alive.

Satan's goal is to snuff out as much of your life as possible.

However, Jesus came so that every area of your life would be filled with light—life and not death. You must come to the understanding that Jesus' goal is life in *every area*. Jesus came to this earth as a human person, endured unimaginable torture, and then overcame death so that *we* could have life.

Not a little bit of life. Not life in only some areas. But abundant life.

God's plan for your life is HEALING. It's FREEDOM**.**

It's *LIFE***.**

If you don't believe that—if there is even the tiniest doubt that it's true—then acknowledge that doubt to the Lord and invite Him to show you the truth.

A word about identity:

Our experiences in life shape how we see ourselves; they help form our identity. God calls us His daughters, but that's not how we see ourselves. We unconsciously feel and act as though we're orphans—unprotected, unloved, uncared for. Yet, growing into a complete understanding of what it means to be God's daughter changes everything in our lives: the way we see ourselves and our place in the world, as well as our relationships with God and others.

Read the following aloud and write out a prayer asking the Lord to help you receive it into your spirit as truth:

As His daughter, I can have confidence that I was CREATED by God, CHOSEN by God, and REDEEMED by God.

Being created by God means He designed me—both my weaknesses and my strengths. All the things I wish were different were designed by Him.

Being chosen by God means he chose me out of my mess. I did nothing to earn it or even ask for it. He chose me in spite of me because of who He is.

Being redeemed by God means that every part of my past—every sin I've committed, every trauma I've experienced, every false word spoken over me—is no longer what controls or determines the course of my life. Thanks to Jesus' work on the cross, my life is now determined by God's love, mercy, and grace.

Principle #4:
Not everything we believe as a result of our sexual abuse experience is true, but the Lord reveals truth to us by His Spirit.

"And you will know the truth, and the truth will set you free."

John 8:32

"When the Spirit of Truth comes, He will lead you into all truth.

John 16:13

Satan's biggest and most effective weapon to use against us is deception. He cannot force us to do anything, but he can deceive us into forming judgments about ourselves and others, including God, that will guide every decision we make and thought we have until those deceptions are displaced.

We'll talk more about this in coming chapters, but for now it's important for us to understand two things.

1. Emotional trauma and wounds lead us to form beliefs about the cause and/or result of that trauma that are based on wrong information. We are all deceived in some way.

2. The Holy Spirit is here to lead us to the truth.

Take a moment to ask the Lord to expose every lie your abuse experience has caused you to believe about yourself, Him, and others. Invite the Holy Spirit to speak truth to your heart to heal the wounds those lies have caused.

Principle #5:
The Lord's heart is turned toward us, not away.

"The Lord bless and keep you; the Lord make His face shine on you and be gracious to you; the Lord turn His face toward you and give you peace."

Numbers 6:24-26

As you walk through your healing journey, it is vitally important that you understand that God's heart is turned toward you. He has ordained this time and provided for it. You are not trying to convince the Lord to do something for you that He doesn't already want to do. You are not trying to earn healing by doing things to please Him. You are not trying to follow a set of magic steps that will result in your healing.

You are simply positioning your heart before the Lord to receive the life and healing Jesus died for you to have. Your healing will come BY HIS SPIRIT.

When you find yourself doubting or questioning the Lord's heart toward you, read Numbers 4:24-26 over yourself:

The Lord blesses me and keeps me.
He makes His face shine on me and He is gracious to me.
The Lord's face is turned toward me, and He gives me peace.

. . . .

The biblical principles outlined is this chapter are the foundation on which the rest of *Sexual Abuse Recovery by His Spirit* is built. Everything you read from this point on will point back to them.

1. Complete emotional healing is possible (Ephesians 3:20).

2. Prayer is essential to emotional healing (Lamentations 2:19).

3. Sexual abuse may affect every area of our lives, but in Christ we have the hope of restoration for them all (John 10:10).

4. Not everything we believe as a result of our sexual abuse experience is true, but the Lord reveals truth to us by His Spirit (John 8:32 and 16:13).

5. The Lord's heart is turned toward us, not away (Numbers 6:24-26).

Integrating each of these principles into your everyday life is a process that may take longer than the time required to read through this chapter, so be prepared to return to these pages any time you find your thoughts or feelings in opposition to them.

Lord, I thank You that Your word is true and that Your promises can be depended upon. May the foundational principles outlined in this chapter be settled in my heart. May my beliefs about who You are and who I am in You be formed by Your word and not by my wounded identity. I submit all my broken places to you, and I invite you to heal them—to restore, redeem, and recover everything that has been lost. **Amen.**

Chapter 2 Discussion

1. Are there specific areas in your life which you find it difficult to believe you could be free and whole? What are they?

_____

_____

_____

_____

_____

_____

2. Write out a prayer telling the Lord how you feel about the promise from Ephesians 3:20. Are you filled will hope for complete healing? Do you have trouble believing the promise for yourself? Tell the Lord what you feel and ask Him to guide your heart in faith.

_____

_____

_____

_____

_____

_____

3. Write your own prayers of confession and invitation that are specific to what you're feeling today:

_____

_____

_____

_____

_____

_____

4. Review the symptoms of low self-esteem described on page 19. Pray over each "yes" answer and anything else the Lord revealed to your heart as you read through this section.

- Acknowledge to Him not only which symptoms you identify with, but also how you feel about having a "yes" answer. Take the time to really pour out your heart to Him.

- Invite Him to bring healing and truth to each area.

- Reject any shame you feel about your self-esteem. Say out loud, "Lord, I reject the shame the enemy wants me to feel. I accept your mercy, grace, and love as You heal my heart."

Write out your prayer:

_____

_____

_____

_____

_____

_____

_____

_____

_____

_____

_____

_____

_____

_____

_____

5. Sometimes we experience inordinate responses to circumstances that remind us of our trauma. These circumstances, known as triggers, can be situations, events, smells, touch, or anything that reminds us of our sexual abuse experience. When you're triggered by something, you likely feel overwhelmed with difficult emotions you can't control, like anxiety, anger, sadness, or numbness. Can you identify your triggers? What are they?

_____

_____

_____

_____

_____

_____

6. What is your response to these triggers? e.g. freezing, anger, panic. Be as specific and detailed as you can.

_____

_____

_____

_____

_____

_____

7. Can you imagine the Lord healing your heart to the point that you no longer experience triggers from your abuse experience? Practice pouring your heart out to the Lord by writing out your answer as a prayer:

_____

_____

_____

_____

_____

_____

8. Do you see yourself as God's daughter, with ready access to the unconditional love, mercy, and grace that His daughter would receive? If not, identify how you believe God sees you, and invite Him to show you the truth.

_____

_____

_____

_____

_____

_____

9. Is it easy for you to imagine that God's heart is turned toward you? Do you struggle with seeing where God was in your abuse experience? How has your abuse experience shaped the way you see God, either now or in the past?

_____

_____

_____

_____

_____

10. Write out a prayer asking the Lord to help you remember that His heart is turned toward you.

_____

_____

_____

_____

_____

_____

_____

11. What other thoughts do you have about this chapter? What else is the Holy Spirit saying to you?

_____

_____

_____

_____

_____

_____

_____

_____

_____

_____

_____

_____

_____

_____

_____

_____

_____

_____

_____

_____

_____

_____

Chapter 3 Meditation Verse

You will keep in perfect peace all who trust in you,
all whose thoughts are fixed on you!

Isaiah 26:3 NTL

Day 1

_____

_____

_____

Day 2

_____

_____

_____

Day 3

_____

_____

_____

Day 4

_____

_____

_____

Day 5

_____

_____

_____

Chapter 3 Daily Prayer

Lord, I ask for a new revelation of what it means to have peace in the midst of difficulty and turmoil. Teach me how to rest in You, how to trust You even when my heart feels broken, and how to keep my hope in Your promises.

Write out anything you hear in your spirit or feel while you pray.

Day 1

_____

_____

_____

Day 2

_____

_____

_____

Day 3

_____

_____

_____

Day 4

_____

_____

_____

Day 5

_____

_____

_____

Chapter 3: Peace and the Pursuit of Healing

I would like to tell you that your decision to purposefully position your heart for healing from your sexual abuse experience has set you on a path filled with joy and respite.

I would like to tell you that receiving healing is easier than you ever dreamed and that the process will be brief and painless.

The truth, however, is much less inviting. Chances are your journey to healing will be hard, possibly harder than you expected. You may face moments of panic, despair, and grief. As you follow the Lord on a journey deep into your heart, into the places you've kept sealed up for years or decades, all while living your normal life and taking care of your normal responsibilities, you'll probably feel overwhelmed.

Often.

You'll probably want to quit. You'll question whether the end is worth the pain, and you'll wonder if it wouldn't be easier to just continue as you were.

So, here's a reminder just in case you've already begun to wonder: It is worth it.

You are worth it.

Redemption is worth it.

Growing closer to the Lord and knowing the joy of walking intimately with Him is worth it.

As difficult as the journey ahead will be, however, we have this promise from the Lord himself:

Peace I leave with you; my peace I give to you.
I do not give as the world gives.
Do not let your hearts be troubled, and do not be afraid.

John 14:27

Often, we see peace as something that God does *for you,* like a supernatural blessing from heaven that you have no control over. And that does happen. We've all heard of people who walked through excruciating circumstances with a peace and calm that could only have come from the Holy Spirit's intervention. Supernatural peace is something the Lord does in us and for us at certain times, and it is indeed a blessing we neither earn nor control.

However, the promised gift in John 14:27 is not a "sometimes" peace, or an "earned" peace. It is *His* peace, the very peace that Jesus himself had. He says, "*My* peace I give to you," then He goes on to say, "I do not give as the world gives." To understand the significance of that statement, let's consider the world's philosophy of provision.

In Allison Lovelace's collection of poetry, *the princess saves herself in this one*, the author tells her life story in a series of free verse poems, and in doing so exemplifies a common worldly philosophy of getting and taking. The author presents her pursuit of happiness and wholeness as though it were a wrestling match between her and the rest of the world, as though every scrap of joy, self-worth, or emotional stability she gains must be wrenched from the fingers of someone who doesn't want her to have it.

This is the same innate philosophy behind envy and jealousy in both the body of Christ and in the world. When I have struggled with envy in my heart toward others, the root of it always comes down to fear: fear that there isn't enough love, attention, provision, or friendship, etc. to go around. That fear would lead me to form a sub-conscious judgment (a statement I believed as fact, even if I never said it aloud) that the other person's happiness, success, or accomplishment somehow affected my own potential for happiness, success, and accomplishment. I subconsciously believed that our lives were somehow a "limited pie" in which a piece for the other person meant less for me.

Envy, then, can be a sign of a deeper issue, the deep-down (unacknowledged, unexplored) belief that physical evidence of God's love and blessing in someone else's life means He has less love for me. That's nonsense for at least two obvious reasons:

1. His love for us cannot be measured by our circumstances.

2. His resources never run out.

His love is *enough* in ways we cannot comprehend with our finite minds. We cannot earn it, and we cannot change it. His love just *is*.

God does not give anything to us the way the world gives. The world would have us all believe we are orphans, working hard to earn or to take from others in order to provide for ourselves because no one else is going to do it for us. But God calls us His children, and He promises to provide for all our needs according to *His* riches and *His* glory, which are limitless[9].

And that includes provision of peace.

His peace—like His love, forgiveness, mercy, and grace—is provided for us in a never-ending supply. He has made it available at all times, in all circumstances, no matter what.

His love is something we don't always *feel*, however. We don't always feel forgiven; sometimes we feel condemned or rejected instead. We don't always feel like His heart is turned toward us, because sometimes it's hard to fathom how it could be. It stands to reason, then, that His peace is the same way. Just as our hearts and minds must be renewed to understand His love and to feel it when we're tempted to feel unlovable, our hearts and minds can be renewed to walk in peace, even when our circumstances are in chaos.

---

[9] Philippians 4:19

Sometimes, peace is a choice we make by faith, and not by sight.

Read the following aloud and then write out a prayer in the space provided asking the Lord to help you receive it into your spirit as truth:

As my Father's daughter, I lack nothing.
His love for me is complete, nothing can be added to it or taken away.
My Father's heart is turned toward me, not away from me.
I am His favorite daughter, and the endless expanse of His love means that others are, too, because His love is more than enough for all of us.

Choosing Peace

Our meditation verse for the week says this:

You will keep in perfect peace all who trust in you, all whose thoughts are fixed on you!

Isaiah 26:3 NTL

I think it's significant that there are no verses in the Bible that say, "You will love those who are faithful and obedient," or "You will forgive those who never make the same mistake again." Yet here is a promise of peace that comes with what seems to be a condition: "You will keep in perfect peace *all who trust in you*, all *whose thoughts are fixed on you*." For one with a shaky understanding of God's nature, it might be easy to assume that the "condition" implies our need to *earn* peace, as in, "If I work hard to keep my thoughts focused on God at all time, He will grant me peace." The opposite is actually true: the peace doesn't come from what we do, but from **who He is.** When we keep our minds fixed on the true nature of God—His true heart for us, His true provision for us—then we can't help but have peace. The magnitude of who God is is so much bigger than our temporary circumstances that peace is inevitable.

Or it would be, if we lived in Heaven, where the eternal light of God's glory obliterates even the faintest shadow of darkness. As it is, our lives are overrun with shadows—fear, insecurity, pain, shame—that are pitch black and all consuming. Most of us have spent our whole lives in those shadows, whether they were cast by sexual abuse or an infinite number of other things. We've also spent our entire lives denying them, unable to face the depth of darkness in which our fear, shame, and pain resides.

Now, however, as we pursue healing and wholeness, we must step into the shadows of our pasts, into the deepest crevices in our hearts, and the pain of it will feel overwhelming at times. Our old patterns of denial, resistance, and self-preservation will undoubtedly attempt to send us running in the opposite direction, and it will take total reliance on the Lord to get us through. We will have to choose, sometimes daily, to continue on our healing journey. We will also have to choose, sometimes daily—sometimes even more—*how* we are going to continue.

Will we drag ourselves by our own strength and force of will down this path to healing?

Or will we walk beside the Lord, relying on Him to hold us up, to rest with us when we need to rest, to show us where to step when the path is rocky, to show us where to go when it becomes unclear?

In other words, will we choose peace?

The obvious answer is *yes, of course I will. I choose peace.* However, we're under no delusions that peace will be an easy choice. Choosing peace means making countless other choices, often in circumstances that make it difficult to see a choice to be made. Choosing peace will require us to guard our thoughts in ways we perhaps never have before, to listen to our hearts more closely than we usually do.

Steps to Choosing Peace

There are certain steps we can take to begin choosing peace over stress, anxiety, and emotional chaos. Calling them "steps" is misleading, of course. Each step is more like a journey all on its own, one that begins with us having to learn to walk all over again: we'll make our first tentative attempts to think in a new way, stumble, fail, try again, make it a little longer this time, then likely fall flat on our face; repeat.

And that's okay.

Choosing peace is not about denying our struggles and powering through, bloody and exhausted, under the crushing weight of how we *should* feel.

I should be able to have peace.

I should be able to rest.

In fact, choosing peace is about the exact opposite.

Choosing peace means choosing to admit our struggles when they arise—our pain, anxiety, insecurity, and fear—rather than ignore them like we've been doing for so long. We do this by pouring our hearts out like water before the Lord[10] and by being real with a safe person, someone who will let us feel what we feel without trying to talk us out of it.

Choosing peace means remembering that everything that steals, kills, or destroys, is from the thief[11], not from God. Anxiety, depression, isolation, fear—the list goes on and on— are from the enemy. They are not "a part of the process." They are not inevitable. They are not weaknesses. They are tactics from the enemy to wreak death and destruction in your heart, and they need to continually be identified as such.

Conversely, choosing peace is about reminding ourselves again and again that **it is okay not to be okay**. As you walk this healing journey, you will undoubtedly face difficult emotional circumstances. Fear, panic, anger, frustration, disappointment—you

---

[10] Lamentations 2:19

[11] John 10:10

are likely to feel them all. You may find yourself exhausted or numb or furious at both God and the rest of the world. When those emotions and emotional states arise, you will be tempted to shame yourself, to revert to "shoulds," but that's the least productive choice.

> I will have peace
> by faith,
> not by sight.

Feeling your feelings *is* productive, even when it feels the opposite. As an abuse survivor, you have spent years, possibly decades, repressing your feelings—not because you're weak, but because that's the normal default response. If your abuse experience happened in childhood, you have likely spent most of your life coping with the consequences of abuse by refusing to feel them. That means you have a lot of feelings swirling around in the deepest recesses of your heart, and they will most likely be overwhelming when they begin to come out.

It's okay not to be okay during those times.

It's okay if your emotions interrupt your daily life.

It's okay. *You* are okay.

Choosing peace, then, is about training our minds to respond differently to our struggles than we've done before. It means identifying our "default response" and then purposefully setting out to change it. For example, when it comes to negative emotions of any kind, my default response—the response I make before I even realize I've responded at all—is denial or dismissal. I shy away from negative thoughts, dismissing them from my mind before they even fully form, and then trudge on as though that thought or fear isn't eating a hole in my soul.

Maybe your default response is shame—you feel ashamed for your struggle, then get sucked into a whirlpool of condemnation and self-recrimination you can't get out of.

Maybe your default response is to exert control over your circumstances, or to escape using media, or to engage in addiction. Whatever it is, purpose in your heart to begin responding differently. Tell the Lord what you believe your default response is and ask Him to help you change it. If you don't quite know what your default response to negative emotional experiences is, ask Him to help you to identify it.

Write out your prayer below.

―――――――――――――――――――――――――――――――――――

―――――――――――――――――――――――――――――――――――

There are a few more things we can do to choose peace.

1. We can learn to recognize untrue beliefs and reject them.

   These beliefs are usually judgments we make by deciding why something is happening or has happened. Sometimes these look like "if/then" statements. For example, during a season when my life was dominated by untreatable insomnia, I had unconsciously made several if/then judgments that kept me in emotional turmoil. One was, *If I can't fall asleep, then the Lord doesn't care about my needs.* I had taken a physical circumstance (not sleeping for days or weeks at a time) and assigned a judgment to it by deciding why it happened (the Lord doesn't care about me). I did not have peace until I acknowledged that judgment and rejected it.

2. We can refuse to assign a negative emotion to difficult circumstances.

   Sometimes circumstances arise that are just hard—disappointing, frustrating, exhausting. When that happens, emotional peace is usually the first thing to go as we grapple with how we feel about what we're walking through. Sometimes there are very real feelings to be worked through, and when that happens, we need to remember it's okay not to be okay. But there are also times that we can choose how we're going to feel. For example, I no longer suffer with insomnia, but there are still times I don't sleep well. When that happens, I have to choose: am I going to get angry, discouraged, or fearful about it, or am I going to accept it for the temporary circumstance it is and move on?

Often, accepting difficult circumstances for what they are *without* deciding that they're something more is a step toward emotional peace.

3. We can intentionally set out to learn the true nature of God, and to understand our place in His heart as His daughters.

I will have peace by faith, not by feeling.

As children of God, we are perfectly secure. No circumstance or emotion can dislodge us from our place in His hand, no "wrong" response can cause Him to turn His heart away from us. He is trustworthy, faithful, and reliable. However willing our spirits are to accept that, though, our flesh is weak and prone to discouragement. The truth of God's love and care for our hearts doesn't always *feel* true, and in those times, we need to accept the truth by faith. In order to do that, our faith in God's nature must be built up beforehand. It's vital that we pursue understanding of who God is so that the truth is settled in our hearts when our flesh begins to doubt.

The following is an example prayer to pray when you face emotional difficulty.

Lord, today I feel [insert your feelings and emotions here; be as precise and detailed as possible].

This is why I feel this way: [spend as much time here as you need to, telling Him all the arguments and struggles in your heart].

I don't know what to do with any of these feelings. But you see my day—my kids, my schedule, and my responsibilities—and you're not expecting me to do more than rest in you. I'm your daughter, and daughters rest, so that's what I'll do.

I'll rest in your love, in the knowledge that your heart is turned toward me, and in your patience and kindness toward me.

I'll rest in the knowledge that you are moving even when I'm hurting, in the understanding that you don't expect me to have all the answers, and in the truth that you're not disappointed in me or my struggle.

I will rest in the knowledge that this is temporary, no matter how it feels, and that you are the one doing the work, because we both know I can't.

I will practice trusting you with my heart, giving you my feelings and struggles, and choosing to believe that it's okay if I don't have it all together today.

I will choose to believe it's okay even though it's hard.

I will choose to believe that if this were not enough, you would tell me, and that if you wanted me to do more than rest, you would make it clear.

I trust you to lead me in wisdom because that's a promise you made to me in your word, and above all things, you are faithful.

Emotional peace in the midst of difficult circumstances is not only a possibility, it's a promise from the Lord Himself (John 14:27). Peace is not something we merely *receive*, however; peace is something we choose. The following list is a brief summary of the steps to choosing peace discussed in this chapter.

- Admit your struggles rather than deny them.

- Refuse to accept anxiety, depression, discouragement, etc. as inevitable, BUT remember that there is no shame in feeling them. What do you do with them?

  1. Submit them to the Lord.

  2. Ask for His intervention.

  3. Ask for the wisdom to know if there are steps you need to take.

  4. **Trust Him** to move on your behalf and **keep trusting** for as long as it takes.

- Remind yourself that it is okay not to be okay.

- Feel your feelings.

- Identify your default response to negative emotional circumstances and purpose to begin responding differently.

- Recognize and reject untrue beliefs.

- Stop assigning negative emotions to difficult circumstances.

- Remind yourself that even the most difficult circumstances are temporary.

- Spend time with the Lord, learning who He is and pursuing His heart.

Lord, I thank You that I can have peace in my heart through this process. I thank you that fear and emotional chaos are not inevitable. Help me to choose peace when my soul is unsettled, when I'm afraid or overwhelmed or unsure. I recognize that choosing peace means choosing to trust You, so I ask You to help me do that more and more. **Amen.**

Chapter 3 Discussion

1. Write a prayer declaring your intention to follow the Lord on this healing journey no matter how hard it gets, how overwhelmed you feel, or how badly you want to give up. Ask Him for the strength, courage, and boldness to continue until the end. Thank Him that your healing is by His Spirit, not by your effort or force of will. Declare your trust in Him. Be prepared to come back to this prayer as often as necessary over the course of this workbook.

_____

_____

_____

_____

_____

_____

_____

_____

_____

2. Do you feel encouraged or discouraged by the idea that you can choose peace? Write out your thoughts.

_____

_____

_____

_____

_____

_____

_____

3. Write out a prayer asking the Lord to help you grow in a right understanding of God's nature.

_____

_____

_____

_____

_____

_____

4. Use this space to make a list of practical things you can do to choose peace. Include both items from this chapter and anything else that comes to mind. Then, on a second piece of paper, rewrite your list and place it where you can see it on a regular basis.

_____

_____

_____

_____

_____

_____

_____

_____

_____

_____

_____

_____

_____

_____

_____

_____

_____

_____

_____

_____

_____

_____

_____

_____

_____

_____

_____

_____

_____

_____

_____

_____

_____

_____

_____

_____

_____

_____

_____

_____

_____

5. What other thoughts do you have about this chapter? What else is the Holy Spirit saying to you?

_____

_____

_____

_____

_____

_____

_____

_____

_____

_____

_____

_____

_____

_____

_____

_____

_____

_____

_____

_____

_____

_____

_____

_____

Chapter 4 Meditation Verse

Arise, cry out in the night, as the watches of the night begin;
pour out your heart like water in the presence of the Lord.

Lamentations 2:19 NIV

Day 1

_____

_____

_____

Day 2

_____

_____

_____

Day 3

_____

_____

_____

Day 4

_____

_____

_____

Day 5

_____

_____

_____

Chapter 4 Daily Prayer

Lord, help me to recognize when I deny my feelings today.
Help me to stop dismissing how I feel, no matter how uncomfortable
it is at the moment. Remind me to bring my feelings to you first.

Write out anything you hear in your spirit or feel while you pray.

Day 1

_____

_____

_____

Day 2

_____

_____

_____

Day 3

_____

_____

_____

Day 4

_____

_____

_____

Day 5

_____

_____

_____

Chapter 4: Confession and Denial

As noted in previous chapters, confession is an integral part of the healing journey. Unfortunately, most of us associate the word "confession" only with sin or wrongdoing, giving the word a negative connotation, but to confess something merely means we *recognize* and *acknowledge* it. Our prayers of confession and invitation are about intentionally and verbally acknowledging our deepest feelings, fears, and desires.

Confession, then, is the opposite of denial, the state in which sexual abuse survivors tend to live most of their lives. We deny the reality of our emotional pain, our struggles, and our needs. We usually don't deny it outright. For example, few survivors would say, "My sexual abuse experience didn't affect me." Rather, we deny it by refusing to acknowledge and confront the ways our sexual abuse experience continues to affect us in the here and now.

> To confess is to ACKNOWLEDGE that our feelings are REAL.

My personal journey from denial to confession is a winding road I've been traveling for years, and I'm still far from arriving—the destination being when I have learned to respond to negative emotions by acknowledging and dealing with them rather than by stuffing and denying them.

Part of that journey included recognizing the damage created by living my life based on shoulds and shouldn'ts. I noticed that my first response to a difficult season was always the same: *I shouldn't be feeling this way*.

I should be over this by now.

I should know better.

Since I didn't believe whatever issue I was facing should actually be an issue, I refused to deal with it, generally for weeks at a time. I would gradually grow more and more miserable, beating myself up the entire time because, by my assessment, I shouldn't have been miserable at all.

Even the strongest emotion-stuffer can't maintain that stance forever, however, and so the time inexorably arrived that I would fall completely apart. There, in a place of abject brokenness, I'd take whatever hurt I had been so intent on denying to the Lord; I would confess it—that is, verbally acknowledge it—either out loud or in my journal. He would speak truth to my pain, and remind me that despite my brokenness, I had no reason for shame. Then my heart, in that area at least, would be healed. I would finish that experience always wondering what I'd been so afraid of. *Why did I put this off for so long? I'm not doing that again.*

Until the next time my damaged emotions were triggered, and I faced feelings and fears I didn't think I should have. When that inevitably happened, the cycle would begin again: pain, denial, brokenness, healing, repeat. Over and over.

For years.

I can't pinpoint exactly when my response to negative emotions began to change, but I connect the shift to a time I was reading through the Psalms for the first time in several years and came to Psalm 42 and 43. They can be summed up by this verse:

> *Why, my soul, are you downcast? Why so disturbed within me?*
> *Put your hope in God, for I will yet praise Him, my savior and my God.*

Psalm 43:5

That question, "Why, my soul, are you downcast?" made me realize that I never stopped to confront or question my negative emotions. Anxiety, depression, fear, insecurity—I just felt them, beat myself up for feeling them, and told myself to get over it, despite this response being ineffective 100% of the time. But after reading the above verse that day, I wanted to respond to my own heart differently. I began to make a list titled "Things I'm trusting God with this week." Whenever I felt downcast or out of sorts, I would journal about everything I was feeling in detail—every emotion I was struggling against and everything I believed about the situation, even if I knew said beliefs were based on a lie. (This is a significant step for me because when I feel something that I know isn't actually true, I tend to tell myself I should know better and then attempt to move on without processing the actual feeling. This is also ineffective 100% of the time). Finally, I'd write out God's truth about the situation. I would write, "I can trust God with this situation because His Word says _____" or something similar.

> Denying the truth of how we feel denies God the opportunity to heal us.

Somehow writing down my feelings—putting them on paper, where I could no longer dismiss or gloss over them—shifted something inside of me. Just as surely as denying my fear and insecurities dragged out my misery, confessing them allowed the Lord to speak truth to them right away, which brought peace. And even when I didn't receive an "answer" in my heart right then, simply declaring that I could trust God with those things brought peace to my soul. I learned that denying the truth of how we feel denies God the opportunity to heal us. We have to invite Him into our reality rather than trying to convince Him (and ourselves) that we live in a different reality altogether.

The second incident that impacted my response to negative emotions was when I came across this by-now-familiar verse:

> *Arise, cry out in the night, as the watches of the night begin;*
> *pour out your heart like water in the presence of the Lord.*

Lamentations 2:19

At first, I only focused on the last part, "*pour out your heart like water in the presence of the Lord.*" As mentioned previously, I pictured my heart as a bucket of water when

I prayed. I could choose to splash a little out in the Lord's direction, or I could choose to pour it all out. I realized I no longer wanted to live feeling like an overflowing bucket of murky, polluted water. I want to live in that clean, emptied-out feeling—in the freedom and security of being fully known by the Lord.

But after a few weeks of meditating on this verse, I began paying more attention to the first line. It says, "Arise, cry out **in the night**, as the watches of the night **begin**." In the context of the scripture, the night watches would have been when soldiers kept guard over the city at night, pacing the walls and watching the surrounding land for invaders or attackers. Night would have been when the city was most vulnerable to all the dangers that may have been hiding in the darkness. Many sexual abuse survivors can identify with that in a literal sense: often the night was when we were most vulnerable as well.

In a broader sense, "night" can be read as a metaphor for times of vulnerability or difficulty in our everyday lives, when we're anxious, grieving, angry, or withdrawn. Yet the scripture doesn't exhort us to merely keep our guard up when we feel vulnerable, as the soldiers would have done for the city. Instead we are told to pour our hearts out like water before the Lord *as the watches of the night begin.* At the first sign of vulnerability, at the first indication of fear or pain or insecurity—THAT'S when we need to go to the Lord.

Two things:

1. We cannot deny our vulnerability and keep guard over it at the same time. If someone came with a wrecking ball and knocked down one of the walls in our home, we would never deny the wall was broken, or pretend the winter wind wasn't freezing us to our bones. Why should our hearts be any different?

2. Being aware of our vulnerability isn't enough to overcome it. We must bring it to the Lord, pouring it out to Him, holding nothing back.

My journey to healing from all the wounds caused by my abuse experience was a roller coaster of denial and confession. I spent 20 years in denial—in an outright refusal or inability to admit the depth of what I felt. I only dealt with the *symptoms* as they became more than I could cope with, never the deeper brokenness. I brought them to the Lord (only ever after the pain-denial-brokenness cycle) and asked Him to heal them. And He did, in bits and pieces, because that's all I allowed Him to touch. It was not until I confessed (verbally acknowledged) all of it—the very depths of what I'd spent years hiding and denying—that I experienced complete healing.

> Confession is a means of God's grace.

I don't begrudge myself those years of denial, just as you shouldn't begrudge any part of your journey. In the wise words of my favorite pastor, "You can't know what you don't know." I could not know what pain and shame was hiding in the depths of my heart until the Lord revealed it, just as you can't. Additionally, I didn't know how to walk out my journey any differently than I was already doing it, and neither did you. Very few sexual abuse survivors have the privilege of seeing someone else openly walk out their healing. As I was walking through all those years, the only person I knew who was talking about their abuse experience was me, teaching about sexual wholeness at church retreats, sharing the bits and pieces of healing I was receiving, telling the truth of my story—a little more each time—as I was able.

Bits and pieces of healing are not a bad thing. Sexual abuse causes so many different wounds, layer upon layer of lies and shame. It's impossible to process all of it at once. It's impossible to process any of it at all, except by His Spirit, which is why the practice of confession is so vital to our healing. When we confess our pain to the Lord and invite Him into it, we're allowing Him to heal us, rather than denying Him the opportunity to do so.

A word about dismissal:

Denial happens when we avoid, hide, or mask our negative emotions or the ways our abuse experience continues to affect us. We know that denying our reality doesn't make it any less real; it simply denies God entrance into our hearts. Confession, on the other hand, invites God into our reality—to intervene, to bring truth, to heal. Confession positions our hearts to receive the healing God wants to do in us. Sometimes we can easily recognize denial at work—when we're willing to admit it, of course. But denial can take many forms. One specific way we deny our feelings is by dismissing them. When you dismiss your feelings, you're telling yourself that they are invalid or unworthy of consideration.

Examples of dismissal:

"What happened to me wasn't as bad as what others have experienced."

- We should never compare our experience to someone else's. Everyone responds to trauma differently, and there is no right or wrong way to do so. Your feelings are *your* feelings; that alone makes them valid, and it is necessary to deal with them as they are, not as you believe they "should be."

"My abuser/failed protector wasn't a bad person. They don't deserve _____."

- Abuse survivors often feel guilty about their response to the trauma of their experience, especially when their abuser or the person who was supposed to protect them was a loved one. We sometimes feel the need to protect our abuser and failed protectors, even from our own feelings. It is vital, however, that we allow ourselves the freedom to feel what we feel. Dismissing or denying our feelings will only prolong our suffering.

I spent years refusing to allow myself to grieve all the things I lost through sexual abuse. Any time feelings of grief or loss arose, I immediately dismissed them, telling myself there was no point in feeling the pain of something that couldn't be changed. Some of those losses were:

- My innocence

- A "normal" life

- The opportunity to know what it meant to be a "daddy's girl"

- My dad

My feelings of loss could not be resolved until I allowed God to walk me through the grieving process. I had to acknowledge the loss I felt, feel it in its fullness, and submit the truth of my feelings (rather than some cleaned-up version that fit the "shoulds") to the Lord.

Denial and Shame

Ultimately, denial itself is a symptom of the much deeper issue of shame. Often, we tell ourselves we shouldn't feel what we feel because, whether we realize it or not, we're ashamed of what we perceive to be weaknesses. Shame says we are bad or wrong for feeling the way we do. It is the filter through which we see ourselves, like wearing glasses that cause everything we see in ourselves to look dirty and disgusting. We rarely stop to consider that we're holding ourselves to a standard to which we are unlikely to hold someone else who has experienced similar trauma. If another sexual abuse survivor were to admit to us the shame they feel about how they responded or continue to respond to their abuse experience, we would probably comfort them with the truth of Romans 8:1,

> *Therefore, there is now no condemnation*
> *for those who are in*
> *Christ Jesus.*

"The Lord does not condemn you," we might say, "and He is not angry with you for the ways you've coped with your broken heart, so why should you condemn yourself?"

But we do condemn ourselves. Our inner voice shames us into silence, into denial, into stuffing our negative emotions as deep as we can for fear of what they might mean—that we are damaged, scarred, irreparably broken.

In this, as in all things, perceived truth *feels like truth*. We may *feel* damaged, scarred, and broken—it may be the perceived-truth we spend decades hiding from—but it is not the truth. Confession is our first step toward allowing the Lord to bring the perceived-truth of our hearts into alignment with who He says we are: His daughters.

I sought after the Lord and He delivered me from all my fears.

Those who look to Him are radiant.

Their faces are never covered with shame.

Psalm 34:4-5

Shame says we are orphans—unable to be loved, cared for, and cherished because we are bad, wrong, dirty, disgraceful. But daughterhood means we are exactly the opposite: deeply loved, dearly held, undoubtedly secure.

Steps to Dealing with Difficult Emotions

Following are five practical steps we can take when faced with a difficult emotional circumstance.

Step 1: **Acknowledge what you're feeling**. Are you feeling anxiety, worry, or insecurity? Anger, grief, or fear? Whatever it is, name it.

Today I feel:

Step 2: **Explore the cause**. What circumstance or situation triggered the feeling? Get as detailed as possible, not only about the circumstance but about how you feel about it. What exactly are you afraid of? What are you grieving? Why are you angry? Do not shy away from any of the thoughts or feelings that come up; follow your thoughts wherever they lead.

I feel this way because:

Step 3: **Get curious about *why* the situation triggered the feeling**. Ask the Lord to help you understand why you feel the way you do. What is the foundational belief beneath the feeling? For example, you may find that your fear is based on the deep-down belief that God won't take care of you, or that people will judge you and find you lacking in some way. You may be grieving a loss because of what you believe the loss says about you. It's important that you understand the foundation of your feelings so you can submit it to the Lord for healing.

My feelings are based on the belief that _____.

Step 4: **Confess it all to the Lord, Lamentations 2:19 style**. Does the Lord know your situation and how you feel about it? Yes. Was the Holy Spirit with you, guiding you through each of these steps? Absolutely. Is confession necessary anyway? Indeed.

Tell the Lord about the situation, how you feel about it, and the foundational belief you discovered. Also, write down or speak out (or both!) God's truth and promises. Did any verses or biblical principles come to mind as you journaled and prayed? Declare those truths over yourself and your situation.

Step 5: **Invite the Lord to continue healing, leading, and changing your heart**. Inviting the Lord to heal you might seem like a step you could skip, but it's not. Invitation is less about giving the Lord the go ahead, so to speak, and more about positioning our hearts to welcome His working—even when it's hard or painful, even when we're scared, even when we'd rather hide. As Jesus said, the spirit is willing, but the flesh is weak. When we say to the Lord, "Your will be done in my heart," we're putting our flesh on notice: *change is coming, whether you feel up to it or not.*

. . . .

Denial and dismissal are two common default responses to negative emotions. We deny our feelings by refusing to acknowledge them. We dismiss them by treating them as invalid. We can overcome the habits of denial and dismissal by practicing prayers of confession. Confession means to *recognize and verbally acknowledge* our thoughts and feelings. The practice of confession brings our feelings before the Lord and allows Him to speak truth to them.

Lord, I ask you to help me overcome denial in every area of my life. Help me to recognize and verbally acknowledge every negative emotion as they arise, rather than denying or dismissing them. I pray that You would help me break my old patterns of dealing with negative emotions. May my heart be filled with strength and courage to embrace vulnerability, knowing that I can trust you to care for my heart exactly as it needs to be cared for. **Amen**.

Chapter 4 Discussion

1. What is your default response when you experience negative emotions?

_____

_____

_____

_____

_____

_____

_____

2. Do you have a tendency to "should" yourself? If yes, write out an example:

_____

_____

_____

_____

_____

_____

_____

3. Do you tend to invalidate your feelings by dismissing them? Write out an example.

_____

_____

_____

_____

_____

_____

_____

4. Write out a prayer asking the Lord to help you recognize when you deny or dismiss your feelings.

_____

_____

_____

_____

_____

_____

_____

5. Have you allowed yourself to grieve the things your abuse experience took from you? What losses do you need to acknowledge and grieve?

_____

_____

_____

_____

_____

_____

6. Write out a prayer asking the Lord to give you the courage to face the parts of your story that make you feel the deepest shame, the parts you've never been willing to share or even admit to yourself – even if you don't yet know what those parts are. Invite Him to expose the lies that are hidden in those places, and to speak truth to them. Ask Him again to heal the deepest parts of your identity, helping you to see what it means to be His daughter.

_____

_____

_____

_____

_____

7. What feelings, emotions, or situations do you need to entrust to the Lord today? Make your list here.

_____

_____

_____

_____

_____

_____

_____

_____

_____

_____

_____

_____

_____

_____

_____

_____

_____

_____

_____

_____

_____

_____

_____

_____

8. What other thoughts do you have about this chapter? What else is the Holy Spirit saying to you?

_____

_____

_____

_____

_____

_____

_____

_____

_____

_____

_____

_____

_____

_____

_____

_____

_____

_____

_____

_____

_____

_____

_____

Chapter 5 Meditation Verse

The thief comes to steal, kill, and destroy.
I have come that you might have life, and have it to the full.

John 10:10

Day 1

_____

_____

_____

Day 2

_____

_____

_____

Day 3

_____

_____

_____

Day 4

_____

_____

_____

Day 5

_____

_____

_____

Chapter 5 Daily Prayer

*Lord, reveal to me the judgments I've made against You, myself, and others,
so that I can break them in Jesus' name and walk in freedom from their influence.
I thank you that freedom and healing come by your spirit.*

Write out anything you hear in your spirit or feel while you pray.

Day 1

_____

_____

_____

Day 2

_____

_____

_____

Day 3

_____

_____

_____

Day 4

_____

_____

_____

Day 5

_____

_____

_____

Chapter 5: Judgments and Agreements

Every experience we have in life, especially the experiences of our formative years, teaches us what to believe about the world, ourselves, and God. The problem, of course, is that, as children, we are not capable of thinking through all the implications of our beliefs. We cannot rightfully determine their truth or validity. We form our judgments based on the limited information our child-view of the world provides; then those judgements stay with us for years, decades, or even our entire lives. We also make inner vows according to our judgments that will then guide our behavior and our self-talk, even in ways we don't understand or realize.

A vital part of our healing journey will be recognizing and rejecting the judgments, vows, and agreements with lies we've made that keep our thoughts and emotions tied to a false understanding of God, ourselves, and the world. We must do as the apostle Paul encourages the church in Ephesians 4:22-24—

> *"**Put off your old self**, which is being corrupted by evil desires*
> *…**be made new in the attitude of your mind***
> *…put on the new self, created to be like God in righteousness and holiness.*

Every aspect of our lives is guided by our inner beliefs, from our self-talk to our emotions to our behavior. Yet we can spend decades not recognizing what those inner beliefs are or understanding how deeply they affect us. The purpose of this chapter is to encourage you to intentionally examine the thoughts of your deepest heart and invite the Lord to bring truth and freedom as He renews your heart and mind.

Judgments

A judgment, in this context, can be defined as an authoritative opinion, or an opinion based on the authority of our experience. A judgment is formed anytime we add a *why* to a *what*. We take an incident (a *what*) and form an authoritative opinion about *why* it happened.

For example, if someone cuts me off in traffic (an incident), I might immediately decide the guy who did it is a run-of-the mill jerk: inconsiderate, arrogant, selfish, rude—that's the *why*. I may even take it a step further and make it personal: that guy cut *me* off because he doesn't think *I'm* worthy of his respect—a judgment not only against the other person, but also against myself, which can be especially damaging if the belief that I'm not worthy of respect is habitual in my self-talk.

It might be hard to fathom how judging a random person in traffic damages our emotions or guides our actions, but examining the same principle at work in other situations makes the potential clear:

Incident: My pastor walked right past me at church without speaking to me.

Judgment: He doesn't value me as a part of the congregation.

Incident: My mother abandoned me as a baby.

Judgment: She left because I'm not worthy of love.

Incident: I was molested/raped/sexually assaulted.

Judgment: I am broken, dirty, or unlovable.

Vows

We make vows based on our judgments when we declare, either internally or out loud, how we will respond to them. For example, if I judge that my father molested me because I "asked for it" in some way, I might make an inner vow to never be alluring to any man ever again. As I got older, such a vow could cause me to worry excessively about how I dress and to be afraid others were judging me based on my appearance. It might also interfere in my marital relationship, causing me to shut down or withdraw when my husband expresses desire for me.

Vows usually start with the words, "I will never":

I will never allow someone close to me again.

I will never trust another man.

Agreements

Similarly to making judgments, we make agreements when we decide that a lie is true. Early in my healing journey, I realized that my childhood abuse experience had shaped my view of myself and God in huge ways. For one, I had agreed with the lie that to desire sexual intimacy with my husband was wrong or shameful. I had also agreed with the lie that God couldn't possibly love me the way He loved others. I never vocalized those beliefs, or even acknowledged them. They were purely internal and subconscious, but they shaped my world view for longer than I care to remember, because when we agree with a lie, our soul—our mind, will, and emotions—becomes tied to it. The lie becomes the filter through which we see the world.

In another example, I once met with a woman for counseling and personal ministry who was in the midst of serious marital problems. As she told me her story, it became clear that all the issues could be traced back to one thing: she'd lost her "voice" in the marriage. Over the years she'd quit speaking up for herself in even the smallest way, so much so that her husband had quit seeing her as a person separate from himself. He no longer saw her feelings, dreams, or desires as important or worthy of consideration. In his mind, she existed only to serve and please him.

Throughout the story, one event kept coming up: a time she had gone against her convictions and followed her husband into sexual sin. She had a lot of shame for the part she played in the sin they committed together. With the help of the Holy Spirit, we realized that she had allowed her shame to silence her. She had agreed with the lie that by choosing to participate in the sin, she had lost her right to speak up for herself. The lie said she deserved her husband's unkind treatment, so she began to submit to it, with disastrous consequences.

If not for the Holy Spirit, I never would have made the connection between her current circumstances and a sin that happened years ago. She had been *living* her story and had never made the connection. Nevertheless, it was real and was ruling her life, unbeknownst to her. So, we prayed over that lie: we rejected it, and asked the Lord to break its power and to restore her voice. What happened in the following few weeks is amazing. She began to hear and follow the Holy Spirit's prompting to speak the truth to her husband. She boldly but lovingly defended herself and her children against his verbal abuse. Now more than a year has passed, and she continues to walk in freedom as a new and changed person. Rather than internalize his criticism as truth, she began to see the lies for what they were, and even when he tries to use them against her, they no longer cause her pain. She still loves her husband, still fights for their marriage, but she does so with a new understanding of her own worth and value.

My personal example:

For the first 19 ½ years of my marriage, I had chronic insomnia. It started on my wedding night and continued unabated, though it varied in severity. Over the years, the Lord healed my heart of one consequence of my sexual abuse experience after another, but my sleep issues remained. The connection between the two was plain to see: my dad only ever abused me after I fell asleep. I would wake up to all manner of rape or molestation, so I quickly learned to do my best to stay awake. Six short years later, on my wedding night, when I found myself sleeping in bed with a man for the first time, suddenly that instinct to stay awake returned—only now I was successful.

Eventually, my insomnia issues reached new levels of severity. At the time, my family was fostering a newborn, who also happened to be our newly-adopted son's baby brother, so needless to say, we were under stress. On a personal level, my heart was in complete disarray. I had finished the year before on a high note: I had graduated with my bachelor's degree, started writing my first book, *From Silence to Stories,* and we finalized our adoption—all in December. I had incredibly high hopes for what the new year would bring, but then our lives got turned upside down by the Lord. He led me to continue staying home rather than beginning a career of some kind like I had always planned to do after graduating from college. He led us to foster our son's baby brother, something we had steadfastly refused to do right up until the child was born. None of what I had harbored vague-but-heartfelt hopes for was panning out.

By July, my soul still hadn't caught up with all the unexpected changes. After yet another series of weakness and disappointments that confirmed the fears I'd been quietly harboring—fears that I'd missed out or lost something irretrievable—I had a completely sleepless night. And then another and another. Then two weeks passed, still with no sleep, even after handfuls of over the counter sleep-aids. Finally, two years passed during which I took further handfuls of prescription sleep medication, yet still only slept 3-4 hours a night.

Fast-forwarding through the melodrama, sleep deprivation, and seasons of severe depression, I arrived at a weekend retreat my church holds twice a year called an Encounter Retreat. By then I was depressed, exhausted, and terrified all the time. In my brain was a constant barrage of anger, self-pity, and accusation against the Lord. I was suicidal, though I hadn't admitted it yet, even to myself. During all the sessions, starting the moment I arrived on Friday night and going on to Saturday afternoon, I could do nothing but bawl.

Not weep quietly with silent tears streaming down my face. Oh, no.

It was a full-on ugly cry, one I couldn't stop and couldn't control. Worse, I couldn't even explain to myself why I was bawling. I felt completely out of control and over-whelmed with grief for things I couldn't identify.

On Saturday afternoon one of the pastors came over after a particularly difficult session. He said he'd been praying, and the Lord had told him that I'd believed the lie that I couldn't be healed. He quoted the verse about Satan going around like a roaring lion, looking for someone to devour[12]. He wanted to pray against that roar, so he called a few other leaders over to lay hands on me and pray.

---

[12] 1 Peter 5:8

It happened almost immediately: my mind quieted. For the first time in weeks, I felt peace.

As the day continued, so did the peace. I was able to be myself for the first time in a long time—laughing, making jokes, praying over others as the Lord prompted.

Later, during a session on vows and judgments—the same session I'd sat through countless times—the Lord prompted me to reject the vow I'd made as a child to *stay awake*. At first, I didn't even want to do it because I was afraid to get my hopes up that it would be the thing to heal me. After a minute or two of arguing with myself, however, I realized that freedom in the spirit realm is just as important as freedom in the natural, regardless of whether it brought the healing I wanted. Nothing dramatic happened when I went to my friend and pastor for prayer. We simply prayed together to break the vow and moved on.

I'd mislead you if I didn't say that the next 6 months were fraught with worsening insomnia, truly severe depression, and continued suicidal ideation. Breakthrough, at least for the depression and suicidal thoughts, came after a month or so, thankfully. Then, over the months that followed, the Lord began revealing to my spirit what it means to be His daughter, a revelation that quickly became my heart's foundation. In August, however, I was still in recovery mode emotionally, and survival mode physically. My sleep issues continued, unaffected by the higher and higher doses of medicine my doctor prescribed, but as a daughter I was learning to trust the Lord, even when it didn't seem like He was going to heal me. I had come to the place where I was okay with being tired, as opposed to being angry and terrified, like I had been before, that exhaustion would be my permanent norm.

Then one Sunday a guest speaker at church preached a message about spiritual warfare that changed my perception of a lot of things at once. One thing he said is that you can't address a spiritual issue physically; spiritual issues have to be addressed spiritually[13]. One thing I knew for sure was that my insomnia issue was spiritual. It couldn't be physical, because no amount of prescription meds helped. It wasn't emotional except that it had been associated with so much fear—fear of not sleeping, fear of having to function for the rest of my life while perpetually exhausted. But as I had

---

[13] See page 79 for further discussion on this topic

learned to trust the Lord with my sleep issues, even the fear had dissipated. There was no longer any emotion connected to my sleep issues at all. All that remained was the spiritual aspect.

I'd always assumed that the Lord would reveal the root of my sleep issues in His timing, but the message that day made me acknowledge how tired I was of waiting. Not only could I not get the message out of my mind, I suddenly felt strongly that it was time to get off all the prescription medication I'd been taking. I had a doctor's appointment that Friday, and I made the decision on Tuesday to tell my doctor that I wanted to begin weaning off the meds. Then, when Friday morning came, I had some unexpected alone time. I used it to journal about the thoughts and feelings I'd been sorting through all week. As I wrote, I asked the Lord to reveal the cause of my insomnia so we could finally deal with it. And do you know what?

He did.

Suddenly I began to remember things I hadn't thought about in years, specific episodes in my childhood where I had to stay awake to be safe. Between the sexual abuse, domestic violence, and verbal abuse, neither my mom's nor dad's home had been physically or emotionally safe, and I had vowed to stay awake many times in order to protect myself and my family. Additionally, I realized I had made judgments that authority cannot be trusted to keep me safe. The Holy Spirit showed me that insomnia was my mind and body's response to having to keep myself safe in so many different circumstances throughout my childhood. I prayed over each of the vows, judgments, and agreements He revealed, breaking them in Jesus' name.

By the time I was done journaling and praying, I knew I had been healed. A few weeks later, after my brain and body adjusted to being completely off meds, I began falling asleep, unaided, for the first time in years.

The beliefs I had formed as a young child in the midst of abuse stayed with me for decades. They guided even the subconscious workings of my brain in ways that I could neither identify nor control. Other deep-seated beliefs can lead to depression, anxiety, or even fears that present like phobias, causing an uncontrollable physical response when triggered.

Some other common examples of vows, judgments, and agreements include:

- "I don't deserve freedom/healing."

- "I can never be fully free."

- "Men/women/authority can't be trusted."

- "My only value comes from sex."

Do not be discouraged if you don't feel or hear a response right away. As you read in my story, from the first moment of revelation (at the Encounter Retreat in March) to receiving the rest of the revelation and breaking the vows and judgements took several months. You can trust the Lord to show you what you need to know in the right time.

What do we do with vows, judgments, and agreements?

- Reject the lie: "I reject the lie I have believed that _____."

- Renounce the vow: "I renounce the vow _____."

- "I break the power of every lie, judgment, and vow over my life in the name of Jesus."

Things I'm Trusting God With Today

1. I trust that He will reveal every lie, judgment, and vow that I've made in the right time.
2. I trust that when the power of those lies is broken in my life, I will have freedom.
3. I trust Him to care for my heart as we walk through this part (and every part) of the healing process.

A word about "spiritual issues":

A spiritual issue can be defined as anything that distorts one's view of themselves or God. The only way to address these kinds of issues is by answering these questions: *Who is the Father and who am I in Him? How does God see me and how do I see Him?*

For me and insomnia, the deep-down belief I held was that I couldn't trust authority to keep me safe, therefore I had to stay awake to protect myself. Though it was true during my childhood in regard to the authority of my parents, as I grew up the lie that I wasn't safe seeped into my spirit and became a part of my emotional foundation. As such, each revelation I received of the Father's love settled onto the understanding that His love wasn't trustworthy. In my deepest heart I did not believe that He or His love could be what they appeared.

In the months and years before the day He healed me of insomnia, the Lord had to rebuild the false foundation on which I had built my life. He removed lie after lie I had believed, replacing them each time with the truth of who He is *as my Father* and of who I am *as His daughter*. With those realities as my foundation, when He revealed the root of the insomnia—the belief that I couldn't trust authority to keep me safe—I was able to receive deep into my spirit the truth that as His daughter, I am safe, cared for, and loved.

I could have told myself those things every day for a hundred years, and it would not have helped me sleep at night. Healing could only come from revelation by His Spirit.

Another example of a spiritual issue is low self-esteem or low self-worth. At various times in my life I have confronted the deep-down belief that I have nothing of value to offer the world. From being a teen who believed sex was what made me valuable to being an adult whose self-respect has been tied to performance and productivity, battling low self-esteem and self-worth have been ongoing parts of my healing journey. Again and again I have circled back around to the belief that I have no intrinsic value aside from what I can produce, a lie that hinders me from seeing myself the way God sees me. It also affects the way I see Him, as if His heart toward me is determined by what I do. If the deep-down truth I believe in my spirit is that God is angry with me, disappointed in me, or that His heart is turned away from me for whatever reason (lies that can enter our hearts in infinite ways), then I filter every event and every emotion through a lens of shame, with the understanding that I will never measure up or be good enough to earn His goodness toward me. Any time this issue arises, I am perfectly unable to feel any differently in my heart and emotions until the truth of who God is and how He sees me is revealed in my spirit.

Of course, not every emotional or physical issue is spiritual in nature. Depression, anxiety, insomnia—all can be caused by difficult circumstances, chemical imbalances, or other issues that need to be treated with time, medication, or lifestyle changes. However, when an issue is chronic or seasonal rather than episodic (that is, brought on by specific events or circumstances), and/or when medical treatments and lifestyle changes are ineffective, chances are that the root is spiritual in nature and should be addressed through spiritual means.

Some of the following suggestions for how to deal with spiritual issues seem pretty obvious at first glance, but their very familiarity makes it easy to overlook their power and significance. Take the time to read through this list prayerfully and thoughtfully, asking the Lord to show you how to apply these principles to your specific situation.

1. **Pour your heart out like water in the presence of the Lord.**

   As previously discussed, nothing can take the place of your participation in your healing through prayer. Spend time communing with the Lord specifically about the issue at hand. Either by speaking or writing, talk to the Lord about every aspect you've identified: when it began, what makes it worse or better, how it makes you feel, etc.

2. **Don't worry about anything...**

   This one is more difficult than it seems, mainly because worry comes so easily and naturally that we're often not aware we're doing it. In this instance, you can prevent worry in at least two different ways.

   First, don't assign more significance or emotion to the issue than it deserves. Neither depression, stress, chronic pain, nor anything else you experience determines your value in any way. They do not mean you are broken, weak, or less valuable than someone who does not have a similar struggle. Reject every judgment you are tempted to make or have made against yourself.

Second, practice truly trusting the Lord for healing. Any time you find yourself beginning to worry or wonder if you'll ever be healed, even if you don't catch yourself doing it until hours or days have passed, remind yourself out loud that you can trust the Lord with your wounds and your healing. His word promises peace that passes understanding to guard our hearts and minds after we have entrusted our needs to Him[14]. If that means entrusting your needs to Him a thousand times a day in prayer, so be it.

Worry is habit we develop over decades; trust is a discipline we can only acquire through true intentionality. Do not write off as impossible the command to not worry. Instead, be ready to do the hard work of renewing your heart and mind for obedience, so that you may experience the promised freedom.

3. **...but in everything, through prayer and petition with thanksgiving, let your requests be made known to God[15].**

   This one is simple: confess to the Lord your need, then invite Him to heal you.

   After that, continue confessing. Continue inviting. Continue trusting. For everyone who asks receives; everyone who seeks finds; and to the one who knocks, the door will be opened[16].

4. **Wait for the Lord.**

   Emotional healing is not often a quick process. Sometimes the layers of pain, shame, and lies are so deep it can take months or years to process them all. I suffered from chronic insomnia for nearly 20 years and spent 15 of them actively seeking God for healing before the work was completed. That doesn't

---

[14] Philippians 4:7

[15] Philippians 4:6

[16] Matthew 7:8

mean He wasn't moving during those years; as I mentioned above, He brought healing to layer after layer after layer of lies and shame during that time. The process of renewing our minds to think, believe, and *feel* the truth can take years, and every part of the process is important. Don't begrudge the peaceful and restful times when it doesn't seem like the Lord is moving. Don't even begrudge the painful, sleepless, or depressed times. Pray through the difficult seasons, rest during the peaceful ones, and remember through it all the declaration and exhortation from the Psalms:

I remain confident of this:
I will see the goodness of the Lord
in the land of the living.
Wait for the Lord;
be strong and take heart
and wait for the Lord

Psalm 27:13-14

. . . .

Making judgments, vows, and agreements can have extensive spiritual and emotional consequences that we might not recognize for what they are, especially if the vow, judgment or agreement was made in childhood. But we have hope for freedom, no matter how long they've been affecting our lives.

We find freedom from vows, judgments, and agreements by confronting and rejecting them.

- Reject the lie: "I reject the lie I have believed that _____."

- Reject the judgment: "I reject the judgment I have made that _____."

- Renounce the vow: "I renounce the vow _____."

- Ask the Lord to restore the emotional ground you have lost.

Lord, I thank You that I can have freedom from every judgment, vow, and agreement with lies I have made. I thank You that I can know the truth—Your truth—and that Your truth sets me free. Thank You for life, for wholeness, for spiritual and emotional growth. Help me to be strong and take heart. Help me to wait patiently for the manifestation of healing You've already begun. Amen.

Chapter 5 Discussion

1. Review the example of an agreement on page 73. Write out your thoughts about the extensive consequences of making judgments and agreements.

    _____

    _____

    _____

    _____

    _____

    _____

    _____

2. Review the author's personal example of judgments on page 74. What thoughts or feelings does this example bring to mind? Write them here.

    _____

    _____

    _____

    _____

    _____

    _____

3. Write out a prayer asking the Lord to reveal any vows, judgments, or agreements you've made with lies that are affecting your physical or mental health.

    _____

    _____

    _____

    _____

    _____

    _____

4. Begin making a list of every vow, judgment, and agreement you've made that comes to mind throughout your healing journey. Pray over each one, rejecting the lies, renouncing the vows, and breaking the power of each judgment in Jesus' name. Be prepared to come back to this list as many times as necessary as the Lord continues to reveal areas in your heart to which He wants to bring freedom.

Real examples of judgments, vows, and agreements:

"I don't deserve to be healed."

"I have to take care of myself because no one else is going to do it."

"I am not worth what Jesus did to heal me."

"Everyone would leave me if they knew who I really am."

"The things I've done make me unlovable."

5. Review "A word about spiritual issues" on page 79. Can you identify chronic physical, emotional, or mental health problems in your life that at the root might be spiritual issues? If yes, explain:

_____

_____

_____

_____

_____

_____

6. Reread Psalm 27:13-14. Can you say that you confidently believe you'll see emotional healing from the issues noted here or any others addressed in this workbook in your lifetime? In the space below, write out a prayer telling the Lord your answer and asking Him to help you in whatever way is necessary.

_____

_____

_____

_____

_____

_____

7. What other thoughts do you have about this chapter? What else is the Holy Spirit saying to you?

_____

_____

_____

_____

_____

_____

Chapter 6 Meditation Verse

He heals the brokenhearted and binds up their wounds.

Psalm 147:3 NIV

Day 1

_____

_____

_____

Day 2

_____

_____

_____

Day 3

_____

_____

_____

Day 4

_____

_____

_____

Day 5

_____

_____

_____

Chapter 6 Daily Prayer

Lord, I'm so grateful that You are my Healer. I thank you that I do not have to live in fear of always being broken, because you have redeemed me according to the promise in Your Word. You have summoned me to You by my name. You have made me yours.

Write out anything you hear in your spirit or feel while you pray.

Day 1

_____

_____

_____

Day 2

_____

_____

_____

Day 3

_____

_____

_____

Day 4

_____

_____

_____

Day 5

_____

_____

_____

Things I'm Trusting God with This Week

_____

_____

_____

_____

_____

_____

_____

_____

_____

_____

_____

_____

_____

_____

_____

_____

_____

_____

_____

_____

_____

Chapter 6: Redemption and Truth

One definition of redeem is to gain or regain possession of something through payment. We understand that Jesus is our Redeemer because He paid the ultimate price for us to be restored to relationship with God. You could say that when sin came into the world, man was lost to God, but He sent Jesus as the necessary payment to redeem us, to purchase us back from the eternal pit to which sin had condemned us. Though the price was paid once and for all, the process of redemption happens throughout our lifetime as God restores each broken part of our heart, each tragic scene in our story, to reflect His will for us on earth as it is in Heaven.

Bless the Lord, O my soul,
and all that is within me,
bless his holy name!
Bless the Lord, O my soul,
and forget not all his benefits,
who forgives all your iniquity,
who heals all your diseases,
who redeems your life
from the pit,
who crowns you with
steadfast love and mercy,
who satisfies you with good.

Psalm 103:1-5 (ESV)

If I look at the whole of my story as an actual story in which I am the main character, one thing is clear: I am not the author. My story, like all our stories, began with the circumstances surrounding my conception and birth, long before I had the autonomy to determine how a single moment of my life would go. Each scene that followed, each chapter, determined a little bit more about the person I would become.

They did not, however, determine the person I would *remain*. God's grace has done that.

I was born into a family in which I am the only daughter. I have four brothers, two older—though one by only 13 minutes, so I'm not sure if that counts—and, eventually, two younger. My parents divorced when I was seven or so. My brothers and I lived with our mom and spent one night a week and every other weekend with our dad. Around the time I was nine, my dad began molesting me. The abuse progressed from molestation to rape and lasted until two years later when I impulsively told a friend at school about what had been happening. The authorities got involved, my father was arrested, and after a trial in which I testified against him, he was sentenced to 420 years, plus life in prison. He was murdered in his prison cell about nine months later.

Before all of that, though—probably around the same time my dad began molesting me—my mom began using sexual slurs and angry insults against me when she was angry. She would often tell me I was a stupid bitch, a worthless slut, and a whore. Her habit of doing so didn't change or lessen when it came to light that I had been sexually abused and continued right up until I got pregnant and married my senior year in high school. Unsurprisingly, at some point her pronouncements about who and what I was took on the weight of truth.

Not at first, though. In my early teens I did my best to resist the identity she was creating for me. I decided that I would not be what she said I was.

I would not be a slut.

I would not be a whore.

The problem was that my circumstances set me up to be just that. The majority of sexual abuse victims become sexually active at a young age, and I was no different. I began having secret boyfriends before I turned 10, many of whom took advantage of my age and vulnerability, though they could not have known how vulnerable I truly was. I got my first "real" boyfriend—the first boy I chose to like—at 13, and within a few months we had rounded first base and were sprinting for home plate. I hesitated when it came to having actual intercourse, though, out of fear that it would hurt (a leftover from my abuse experience) and because, like any "good" girl, I believed sex before marriage was wrong. However, one thing I had learned from my sexual abuse experience was that resistance was pointless and saying "no" would get me nowhere. So over time, as my mother's words continued to smash their way into my heart, confirming everything I feared about myself, I came to believe I was wasting my time trying to fight the inevitable truth: *I was a slut and a whore.*

I remember the exact moment I embraced that fact of my identity. I was 16 years old, standing in the back room at my job at a fast food restaurant, smoking a cigarette—another thing I'd swore I'd never do. The thought hit me that everything I had been taught to "save" had been taken from me, not to mention the choices I'd made since then to give it away. So what was the point in even trying to resist? What was the point in denying the truth of who I was? So, though I had been sexually active to various degrees for 3 years or more, from that point on, something inside me changed. Sex became a thing to me—a thing I didn't resist or feel any compunction toward whatsoever, a thing I didn't feel anything at all toward, actually. I continued to do it whenever it was expected, but it no longer touched my heart.

Looking back now, I can see God's grace at work in my life, because it's only a short trip from giving up my convictions against sex to giving up my convictions against drugs and alcohol. I shudder to think about where I could have been headed. But a few short weeks later, I was in a car accident that brought an old boyfriend back into my life, and God used those circumstances to rescue me. He didn't allow me to continue destroying myself as I would have done if left to my own devices. A short 11 months later I got pregnant (by the grace of God), we got married (by the grace of God), and together we have been transformed by the grace of God over the course of 2 decades of marriage.

Common themes in a sexual abuse survivor's story:

- Low self-esteem
- Major depression
- Anxiety
- Self-harm
- Self-destructive behavior
- Suicidal ideation
- Sexual dysfunction
- Traumatic flashbacks
- Sleep disturbance
- Irrational fear

After I got pregnant and married, the external evidence of my internal identity lessened bit as I lived the young married life. I was faithful to my husband and happily raised our two children. We found our church home and dove straight into the vision that "every member is a minister." Sitting in the sexual wholeness session of my first Encounter Retreat, listening to the speaker share how God had transformed her heart, I knew I wanted to do what she was doing; I wanted to share my story. I had never heard anyone else talk about their sexual abuse experience, and I had no idea how high the statistics of victimization were, but I knew in my heart that it was something we needed to talk about. After the retreat, my husband and I went on to the Discipleship 201 class and then the School of Ministry, a class designed to equip every member of the body to minister to others. Before I even finished School of Ministry, I had started my own LIFE group. I was on the prayer team and I taught in kids church. At my 6th Encounter Retreat I went as a small group leader and then a few retreats later as a teacher, and I told my story at every retreat for seven years, ministering love and healing to women who desired wholeness in their broken places.

From the outside, I was the poster child for the church's vision that every member is a minister. I did all the things good Christian girls do: I read my Bible daily, I learned to pray out loud, I served in my spiritual gifts, I was open with my story. On the inside, however, I was terrified. Terrified of being exposed, as though at any moment God was going to remember that I was trash—that He didn't love me, didn't want me to serve Him, didn't want to have anything to do with me. Everything I did, I did to please God and to please my church leaders. I did it because they believed in me and because maybe if I didn't do it, they would know I was a complete fraud.

As strong as my fear was, however, it wasn't something I ever actually explored. It was just there, underlying everything I thought and did. Most days I could keep up the ruse that I was the same on the inside as the outside with no problem. But any time the Lord prompted me to step out in a new way—something He did with unbearable frequency—I faced that prompting with crippling insecurity. I've shared before how my path to healing has been a cycle of pain, denial, brokenness, submission, and *then* healing—repeat. Often that pain was precipitated by the prompting of the Holy Spirit to step out of my very narrow comfort zone. Even though I wanted to do the things I felt prompted to do—pray out loud, lead a small group, go to Encounters as a leader, share my story, minister to others—the voice in my head always said the same thing: *Who do you think you are? You can't do that. You're not a leader. No one would want you to do anything if they knew who you really are.* The very idea that the Holy Spirit wanted to dwell in *me*, use *me*, speak through *me* was preposterous. That was for other people, even *every other* person, but it couldn't be true for me.

Yet time after time, the Lord challenged me, encouraged me, and made me able to step into the thing He was calling me to.

Inevitably, I would go through the process again, however. And again and again. For years and years and years.

While there are several defining chapters in my story, events that led me to healing and redemption, the most important one began in 2009, when I became friends with my Aunt Nadine. My mother's oldest sister, Aunt Nadine had lived out of state since long before I was born, and I only knew her from her visits to my grandmother's over the years. She moved back to our home state for good in 2007, and then a few months after my grandmother died in 2009, I stopped by her house one day on a whim. We visited for a few minutes, and she invited me to come back for lunch the next week. So began a friendship that would literally change everything in my life.

I had no way of knowing how much I needed it at the time, but my Aunt Nadine became the first woman in my family to ever *like* me. My mom and grandma loved me, of course, as did my other aunt, but they didn't really know me well enough to like the person I was. We spent time together on their terms, and though they asked questions about my life, it was always in the context of small talk rather than genuine interest. I never considered any of those distinctions important at the time, and probably wouldn't even now, except Aunt Nadine proved to be so different. She *wanted* to get to know me. She wanted to spend time with me—and not just an hour or so for lunch every week. After we had lunch together that first time, we began a weekly ritual that everything else in both of our lives revolved around. I showed up at her house at 10 a.m. every Thursday—or Tuesday or Wednesday or whichever day my college schedule allowed, because she was more than happy to change her weekly schedule based on mine—where she would meet me with a glass of peach-vanilla iced tea. We would cook lunch together, make dessert, work the Sunday crossword, and spend several hours just being together. We talked about everything in our lives, from the mundane to the significant. And the best thing was that she both listened to and remembered what I had to say. She never failed to follow up from one week to the next, and I didn't have to explain the circumstances to her every time. I would rush out the door at 3 p.m., staying until the very last minute I could and still be home when the school bus arrived with my children.

Over those two years, Aunt Nadine unintentionally taught me something I didn't know I didn't know: *I am lovable*. This was years before God started healing my identity, even years before I knew my identity needed healed. I was still deeply immersed in the "pain, denial, brokenness, submission, healing" cycle, with no clue that there was a deeper wound in my heart that God wanted to heal. As I said, I didn't know yet that I didn't believe myself to be lovable. I didn't know how deeply I disbelieved that anyone could or would choose to love me, but it was a marvel to me when Aunt Nadine did.

When she died unexpectedly in 2011, I was devastated. The last time I spoke to her in her hospital room, I remember having the thought, "If you die, who's going to love me?" I didn't know how deeply rooted that question was, or how truly I believed that the answer was "no one," but over the next several months, I grieved so much more than the loss of my aunt. Without realizing it, I was grieving the loss of love from my life, specifically the loss of God's love. All of the crutches I'd used to prop up my identity began to be broken and cast aside, and the deep-down fears I'd been covering with performance for years became exposed. I could no longer "pull my weight" as a Christian—couldn't serve, couldn't pray, couldn't read my Bible, couldn't even stand upright during worship. The inner question, "Who is going to love me now?" transformed over time into the firm belief that no one, including my husband, would love me anymore if they *knew me*.

If they truly knew me, they would choose to walk away.

I won't get into all the melodramatic details, but all the devastation in my inner life eventually led me to see the family-life pastor at my church, Lynné. I could no longer deny there was something broken in me, and I had finally run out of energy to pretend that it wasn't, especially in regard to some sudden and irrational fears that plagued me in my marriage. As a part of the counseling and ministry Lynné does, she told me to write my story, this time not leaving anything out. This wasn't the "write the helpful and shareable parts of my story" exercise that I had been doing for years at retreats. It was more of a "write the parts I'd never told anyone, the parts that made me sure I was a worthless piece of trash" kind of exercise.

So, I did. I admitted to a homosexual relationship I'd had with a friend beginning well before I began being sexually abused—something I had never told anyone before. I wrote about how it felt to be awakened by rape, to scream and cry for help in an apartment full of people and have no one come to save me. I wrote about the guy I had sex with when I was 16 just because I knew he wouldn't call me again, and about how I had tried so hard and failed at not becoming the slut and whore my mom always said I was. And, most significantly, I wrote about the secret shame I had carried since childhood because I had enjoyed some of the things my dad did to me during the abuse. They had felt good, and I knew that meant that I was a gross, disgusting, smear of filth.

As I heard one of my pastors say once, shame is more than knowing you have a problem. It's believing you ARE the problem. And I knew, deep, deep down, that in everything in my life, *I* was the problem.

This is why writing our stories matters: I didn't know how I felt or what I believed about any of those things before I wrote them down. Every one of the beliefs and judgments I had formed about myself throughout my childhood had been so deeply repressed and desperately avoided that I could do nothing but live the consequences, while never understanding that they were the consequences of anything. I believed I was just the way I was, always had been, and probably ever would be. I never knew that my extreme insecurity, the belief that I shouldn't even want to minister or pray or help others, or my connection between performance and value was rooted in the deep-down belief that, at my core, when everything else was stripped away, I was a bitch, a slut, and a whore, and nothing else.

I can't even tell you that going through my story with Lynné was the moment I figured all of that out, but it was the first step. As I wrote it the Lord had begun revealing those deep-down beliefs for what they were: lies. In sharing my story with Lynné, He revealed the truth that I am not only lovable, I am indeed loved for who I am. He had *chosen* me. In sharing my story with my husband for the first time, I was able to open the door for healing *for both of us* and for emotional intimacy like we'd never experienced before.

The Lord began revealing many of the lies in my heart at that time in 2011, and He would continue doing so for years. It wasn't until 2013 that He showed me my true beliefs about my identity, and it wasn't until 2017 that I began to understand what it means to be His daughter. The lies I believed about who I was were so deep and so pervasive that they were the foundation of every relationship, every emotion, every word, thought, and action I took and had taken since childhood. My identity—the character of me in my story—had been written by lies, but God was rewriting it. He rewrote me. He rewrote *my story*, so that even though the circumstances are still the same, the deep-down foundational truths I learned from the events have totally changed. Where once I *knew* I was stupid, useless, worthless trash, I now *know* that at my deepest core, when everything else is stripped away, I am His daughter.

And finally, I understand that being His daughter *is enough*.

I don't have "be" a ministry leader. I don't have to "be" a writer. I don't have to have it all together, look good on the outside, be healed or whole or put on a good face. I can just be me, His daughter, and embrace all of me, even the parts I'd denied or been ashamed of for so long.

I can be depressed or anxious and still be His daughter. I can be exhausted from sleeplessness and still be His daughter. I can lose my temper at my children or be harsh and critical toward my husband; I can hear the same old lie in my head—*Who do you think you are?*—and be tempted to allow the fear of judgment to stop me from obeying the Lord's prompting, but none of that changes *who I am*.

Because I am His daughter. I am His wholly *redeemed*—bought back from the pit of lies and shame to which my sin and the sin of others had condemned me—daughter.

And that is enough.

Writing your story

Now it is time to begin writing your own story. There is no timeline for this exercise, so if it takes you 15 minutes or you continue working on it for several months, that's okay. Since the prospect of writing our stories can feel daunting, here are a few guidelines to help you get started. Come back to this page any time you feel stuck as you write.

Pray first. Every time you sit down to work on your story, pray and ask the Holy Spirit to guide your thoughts and to bring clarity and truth to any lies you have believed.

Be honest. You are writing your story solely for yourself, so there is no reason to censor it in any way. God is your only audience, and He already knows it all. Do not write what you think you *should* feel, or what you would want others to take from it; write only the truth of what you felt at the time and what you feel now, if it has changed.

Do not merely list the events. Your story is about so much more than the things that happened to you. It is about the feelings you experienced, the judgments you made about yourself, God, and others, and about the deep beliefs that formed you as a person.

Reject distractions. Do not get caught up in worrying about *how* you write your story, whether or not the narrative would make sense to someone else, or imperfect grammar and handwriting.

Reject fear. Do not allow fear to prevent you from beginning. For example: fear that someone will violate your privacy and read your story without your knowledge, fear that it won't make sense, etc.

Reject stress. Do not stress about where in your timeline to start or what to include. When you begin to feel stress or anxiety, pray over it, asking the Lord to calm your fears and help you to rest in the knowledge that He is guiding you.

Reject limits. Do not limit your story to your sexual abuse experience. Include every external and internal event that shaped you into who you are or were.

When you have finished your story, seek out a safe person with whom you can share it. This might be a pastor, a mentor, or a close friend who is also a spiritually mature, growing Christian. Pray for the Lord to lead you to the right person if no one comes to mind, and also pray for the courage to follow through.

Lord, I want to thank You for the promise of redemption. Thank You for redeeming my life from the pit to which my sin and the sins of others condemned me. I thank You that there is no part of my story that cannot be rewritten, no wound that cannot be healed, no lie that cannot be displaced with the truth. I thank You that I am Your daughter and that is enough, and I ask You to continue settling the truth of it deep in my heart. As I write my story, I pray for the courage to confront every lie, every judgment, and every fear, and I invite you to eradicate shame from every area of my heart. Continue to show me what it means to be redeemed by You, to draw strength from You, and to trust You with my story. **Amen.**

Chapter 6 Discussion

1. Write out Isaiah 43:1 in your favorite translation. What stands out to you the most from this verse? Write out your thoughts or a prayer.

_____

_____

_____

_____

_____

_____

2. How might writing your story help you? Write out your thoughts.

_____

_____

_____

_____

_____

_____

3. Can you identify with the statement, "Shame is more than knowing you have a problem. Shame is believing you are the problem"? Write out your thoughts.

_____

_____

_____

_____

_____

_____

4. One of the biggest lies abuse survivors believe is "I'm the only one." Sometimes it takes the subtle form of a belief that we're broken in ways no one else is. Other times it sounds like "should": *This should not be an issue. I should be over this by now.* Can you identify specific thoughts, feelings, or struggles that made you believe you're the only one who has felt that way?

_____

_____

_____

_____

_____

_____

_____

5. Review the list you made in chapter 1 of everything you want God to do in your heart during this group. Is there anything you'd like to add? Spend a few minutes praying through the things on your list.

_____

_____

_____

_____

_____

_____

_____

_____

_____

_____

_____

_____

_____

6. As stated in the first paragraph on page 91: "One definition of redeem is to gain or regain possession of something through payment. We understand that Jesus is our Redeemer because He paid the ultimate price for us to be restored to relationship with God. You could say that when sin came into the world, man was lost to God, but He sent Jesus as the necessary payment to redeem us, to purchase us back from the eternal pit to which sin had condemned us. Though the price was paid once and for all, the process of redemption happens throughout our lifetime as God restores each broken part of our heart, each tragic scene in our story, to reflect His will for us on earth as it is in Heaven."

Think about the definition and the examples of redemption given in this chapter. What might redemption look like in your story? What do you hope it will restore in you? What specific "pit" are you thankful the Lord brought you out of?

_____

_____

_____

_____

_____

_____

_____

_____

_____

_____

_____

_____

_____

_____

_____

7. What other thoughts do you have about this chapter? What else is the Holy Spirit saying to you?

_____

_____

_____

_____

_____

_____

_____

_____

_____

_____

_____

_____

_____

_____

_____

_____

_____

_____

_____

_____

_____

_____

_____

_____

Chapter 7 Meditation Verse

Though one goes along weeping, carrying the bag of seed,
he will surely come back with shouts of joy, carrying his sheaves.

Psalm 126:6 (HCSB)

Day 1

_____

_____

_____

Day 2

_____

_____

_____

Day 3

_____

_____

_____

Day 4

_____

_____

_____

Day 5

_____

_____

_____

Chapter 7 Daily Prayer

Lord, today I ask for new courage and renewed strength to continue this healing journey. I know that on my own I can only become weak, tired, and exhausted, but as I trust in you may I find new strength. May I run and not grow weary. May I walk and not faint.

Write out anything you hear in your spirit or feel while you pray.

Day 1

_____

_____

_____

Day 2

_____

_____

_____

Day 3

_____

_____

_____

Day 4

_____

_____

_____

Day 5

_____

_____

_____

Things I'm Trusting God with This Week

_____

_____

_____

_____

_____

_____

_____

_____

_____

_____

_____

_____

_____

_____

_____

_____

_____

_____

_____

_____

_____

_____

_____

Chapter 7: Freedom from Shame

As noted in the previous chapter, shame is more than knowing you have a problem. It's believing you ARE the problem. In other words, shame is the difference between "I did a bad thing" and "I am a bad thing."

In my own story I have had three life-changing confrontations with shame. The first, discussed also in Chapter 6, was when I wrote my story and shared it with my friend and pastor Lynné. The things I admitted and acknowledged in my story had kept me bound up in fear of exposure, fear of rejection, and the deep-down knowledge that I was the worst kind of human scum for over twenty years. Confronting it that day broke its power over my life, setting me on a new course—a new trajectory of freedom.

It's worth noting, however, that if you had asked me before I began writing my story, "Emily, do you have shame connected to your abuse experience?" my answer would have been a quick and confident, "*Of course not!*" After all, I had no reason to feel ashamed. What my dad did wasn't my fault, et cetera et cetera. So, no. No shame.

The second time I was confronted with major shame was when I published my first book, *From Silence to Stories*. The whole premise of the book is that it is vitally important to both the sexual abuse survivor and to the world at large that she tell her story. Yet, putting *my* story out there for the world to see elicited intense feelings of fear and shame. Thankfully, the Lord had already led me to stop letting fear make my decisions or I never would have followed through, but after the book was *out there,* my fear intensified a hundred-fold. I began waking up in the night in heart-pounding, gut-wrenching panic. I even had nightmares where everyone from my close friends to my most distant acquaintances ran away from me in disgust (in one dream I had a gigantic spider on my face…how's that for a perfect metaphor?). I was terrified of judgment, of being thought of as *that* girl—the girl with the disgusting sexual abuse story that she wouldn't shut up about—and overwhelmed with shame about what being that girl said about me.

In a culminating moment, one Sunday about two weeks after the publishing date, I went to a sweet friend and spiritual mama for prayer. My choices had narrowed to either asking for help or collapsing to the floor in front of my entire church to weep, so I made (what I hoped) was the least embarrassing choice. On my way up front where the prayer teams were waiting, however, I broke into a run. I threw my arms around my friend's neck when I reached her and bawled—quite loudly, quite *wetly*—into her hair. In between sobs I admitted out loud for the first time the over-whelming fear and shame that had been building for weeks.

She did the only things she could have done in that moment: she held me as I wept; she listened, she prayed, she loved me just like I needed. Throughout the rest of the day the Lord spoke truth after truth to my heart—reminding me that publishing *From Silence to Stories* was His plan, that my story is His story, and that I am safe and secure with Him. Then finally that night at a monthly worship and ministry gathering, we sang a song that included this line[17]: "Your love is proud to be seen with me." Though I had heard the song many times before, in that instance it spoke straight to my heart.

My Heavenly Father is not ashamed of me.

He is proud of me.

He is proud to call me His daughter.

Even when I am embarrassed to be seen with me, He never is.

As the truth of those words sunk deep into my soul, every last vestige of fear and

---

[17] "Pieces" by Bethel Music

shame fell away. The truth of God displaces every lie, including fear and shame; it leaves no place for them.

But again, if you had asked me if I had shame about my story before any of those things happened, I would have told you, unequivocally, "Nope, no shame. Haven't you read my book? The Lord has healed me of all that."

The third time I came up against hidden shame was not related to my sexual abuse experience at all. It began with a frustrating and difficult evening at home that led to an unexpected argument with my husband. I'll spare the gory details, but it all culminated with me needing to apologize for some things. No big deal, right? I'm a grown-up person, spiritually and emotionally mature. Immediate, heartfelt repentance is my go-to response to wronging someone.

Everyone, that is, except my husband. When confronted with something I said or did that hurt him or was a sin against him, my go-to response had long been deflection: blame, anger, fault-finding. This particular day, for the first time in 20 years of marriage, my husband called me on it. He pointed out that I owed him an apology and expressed how my refusal to repent made him feel. As I listened, I was overcome with shame for the kind of wife I had been all those years. I felt selfish, demanding, and ungrateful. Irredeemable, as though the inherent flaws that made me the kind of wife I was could not be changed or fixed, even by the Lord.

With many tears, I apologized for what I had said and done in that particular instance, but I couldn't look him in the face for the rest of the night and into the next day. I was overwhelmed with shame. Buried in it. Knowing shame as I do, I spent the day journaling through the experience to try to find the truth in it, but I kept having to hide in the bathroom to weep. I could not shake the thought that I always had been and always would be a terrible wife, not worthy of my husband. Nothing could change my inherent selfishness. No matter how hard I tried I would always be a broken, horrible wife.

No exaggeration: that feeling lasted a full 24 hours.

> Though one goes along weeping, carrying the bag of seed, he will surely come back with shouts of joy, carrying his sheaves.
>
> Psalm 126:6 HCSB

The next morning, I awoke with a clearer head and a new understanding of what had happened the day before. First, I recognized for the first time that the difficulty I'd always had repenting to my husband was connected to the shame I felt about who I had been as a wife early in our marriage. I had treated my husband the same way I had seen husbands treated as a child: with constant contempt, derision, and dishonor. As I grew spiritually and learned how to be a godly wife, I was embarrassed and ashamed of my previous actions, but I wasn't emotionally mature enough to voice repentance to him. Shame said I was flawed, selfish, irredeemable; to my thinking, repenting to him for my failures would have drawn attention to that fact, leaving him with no choice but to stop loving me. So instead, I spent the next 20 years casting blame and finding fault in him any time I did something wrong, and every time, my inability to repent confirmed the lie that I was deeply flawed and selfish, compounding my shame and strengthening my inner fear of exposure.

So the cycle continued.

Second, I understood more about how shame operates than I ever had before. The lie about my identity as a wife was too painful to contemplate, much less confront, so any time I had gotten too close to it over the years, I immediately—unconsciously—responded to it in whatever way I could to avoid feeling it. So, if you had asked me, "Emily, do you have shame about who you are as a wife?" I would have honestly, sincerely responded "No, of course not." I had spent so much time and emotional energy avoiding the things I was ashamed of that I never even recognized the shame I felt. Like a ball in a pinball machine, I bounced away from my shame-triggers so fast I didn't even know what I had bounced away from. Rather than identify what I was feeling as shame, I avoided it with anger, control, fault-finding, performance, or perfectionism—thereby creating more shame, more pain, and a stronger urge to avoid it.

Third, I understood why the Lord hadn't *removed* my shame during that 24 hours of misery, why I continued to feel it even after recognizing it. Even better, though, I now knew without question what I needed to do about it.

Understanding Shame

Before we can begin truly overcoming shame in every area of our lives, it's helpful to understand how it operates. Let's look at a couple of ways shame can enter our hearts: through a sin (or perceived sin) we've committed, or through a judgment we've made.

Shame from sin begins with a misapplication of God's love, mercy, and forgiveness. Often, the sins we're most ashamed of happened before we were spiritually mature enough to apply the truth of His love to ourselves. We may have known cognitively that salvation equals forgiveness, but deep down we didn't understand what it means to be forgiven. As we grow spiritually, the shame we feel about those sins prevent us from getting close enough to them to apply the truth of God's love and the revelations of His grace we've received. As in my story, both the sins I'd committed in the aftermath of being sexually abused and the perceived "sin" I'd committed by at times enjoying the abuse, as well as the sins I committed against my husband early in our marriage, were all so shameful to me that I couldn't do what I knew to do to deal with sin: confess and repent.

Shame can also enter when we make a judgment against others or ourselves. We can form judgments against ourselves because of our sin—based on my sin and perceived sin, I judged that I was irredeemably broken and unforgivable, for example. The thought was so painful that I couldn't get close enough to the sins to actually deal with them. As discussed in Chapter 5, we also can form judgments based on trauma or other damaging experiences, e.g. *What happened to me was my fault.* And we can form judgment based on outright lies, ones we either heard spoken over us or that stemmed from our own wounded hearts. For example, when I felt overcome with shame after publishing *From Silence to Stories*, the root came down to a judgment I had made years before, back when fear was still making my decisions. Any time I saw someone "putting themselves out there" in pursuit of their dreams, I would inwardly respond in two ways: envy and judgment of their motives—*wow*, I would think, *need attention much?* I subconsciously devalued the person and their dream because of what I deemed as their attention-seeking motives. Over time, the Lord healed my heart of all the wounds that caused my envy and judgments, but the judgments themselves continued to be the filter through which I perceived my own actions (because that's how judgments work). In my heart, "putting myself out there" made me expect everyone to judge my motives and value the same way I had judged others'[18], and the thought of being valued so lowly by people I loved and respected brought shame.

Overcoming Shame

With a better understanding of how shame enters and operates, we can take the necessary steps to deal with it in a way that brings freedom, healing, and spiritual growth.

Step 1: **Confront shame.** Shame sets us on a continual path of pain, avoidance, and more shame. Because our shame-feelings are so strong, we avoid them and the underlying sin/judgment at all costs. But to overcome shame, we have to experience it. Explore it. Allow it to expose all its lies. Though each of my three major confrontations with shame looked different on the outside, they all included a period of *feeling* it—no more denial, no more avoidance. I had to sit in it, feel it, stay with it long after my soul was ready to be done.

They say the first step is the hardest, and that's definitely true in this case.

Step 2: **Identify the origin.** Did shame enter through a sin you committed? A lie you believed or a judgment you formed against yourself? Like any weed, shame about who I was as a wife started from an actual seed: sins against my husband early in our marriage. Shame began with sin (bad things I'd done), but quickly grew into the belief that *I* was the bad thing. In order to deal with it biblically, I had to identify both the sins at the root of my shame and

---

[18] Not only is this a perceived truth, it's also a biblical principle. Luke 6:37-38 explains that when we give judgment, we receive it back—pressed down, shaken together, and running over into our laps.

the sins I'd committed since then in my attempts to avoid shame's exposure.

Step 3: **Confess and repent.** This might look different depending on how shame entered. If it's from a judgment you formed against others or yourself, including judgments formed based on perceived sin, confess that judgment to God[19] and to a safe person[20]. Reject the judgment as truth and turn from it.

If shame entered through sin, confess and repent not only to the Lord, but also to the one you sinned against. In my case, I had to go to my husband and acknowledge not only the ways I'd sinned against him in our early years of marriage but also all the ways I'd sinned against him by refusing to repent through all the years that came after. I have to admit, this step took me a few days to complete, but it *had to be completed.* To refuse to confess and repent would have been yet another sin against him and would have only perpetuated the cycle.

Confession and repentance are the means of God's grace and mercy to break the cycle of shame. If for some reason confession and repentance to the person you sinned against truly isn't possible (as opposed to just being scary or uncomfortable), go to a pastor or other spiritual authority in your life to confess and repent. **You cannot successfully overcome shame while still allowing it to reign.**

Step 4: **Reject shame and pray to break its power in Jesus' name.**

Lord, I reject the shame I've felt about _____. I recognize that shame is not the truth. I submit to you these feelings of shame and ask that their power to rule my life be broken in Jesus' name.

Step 5: **Act in the opposite spirit.** Now that the power of shame has been broken in your life, you can choose how you respond to each new opportunity that arises for you to feel shame. You no longer have to hide, deny, or avoid it. You can choose to respond to shame with confession and, when needed,

---

[19] 1 John 1:9

[20] James 5:16

repentance. Each time you do, you will be choosing light over darkness, wholeness over brokenness, and truth over the most crippling of lies.

. . . .

The amazing thing about all of this is that shame *can be* overcome, no matter how long it's been around or how deeply entrenched it is. That doesn't mean you will never experience shame again—as evidenced by my own story—nor does it mean you will never struggle with taking the necessary steps to overcome it—also evidenced in my own story. But the presence of shame is not indicative of anything except your humanity; it is the normal and expected response to real or perceived wrongdoing[21]. In other words, feeling shame is nothing to be ashamed of. It is merely a feeling to be confronted and, gloriously, defeated, as you continually grow in healing and freedom by His Spirit.

The closing prayer is taken from Romans 8:31-18.

God, if You are with me, who can be against me? You, who did not even spare your own Son but gave Him up for me, how will You not now graciously give me all things? Who can condemn me? No one, because the One who died for me was also raised to life and now intercedes for me at Your right hand. Who can separate me from Your love? Should trouble or hardship or persecution or famine or danger or sword? No, because in all these things I am more than a conqueror through Him who loves me. For I am convinced that neither death nor life, neither angels nor demons, neither the present nor the future, nor any powers, neither height nor depth nor anything else in all creation will be able to separate me from Your love. **Amen.**

---

[21] For more on overcoming shame, read *Daring Greatly* and/or *Rising Strong* by author Brené Brown.

Chapter 7 Discussion

1. As you read this chapter, did any sins you've committed, judgments you've made, or beliefs you've formed about yourself come to mind that have opened the door to shame?

_____

_____

_____

_____

_____

_____

2. Use this space to journal as you walk through each of the 5 steps to overcoming shame.

_____

_____

_____

_____

_____

_____

_____

_____

_____

_____

_____

_____

_____

_____

_____

_____

3. What other thoughts do you have about this chapter? What else is the Holy Spirit saying to you?

_____

_____

_____

_____

_____

_____

_____

_____

_____

_____

_____

_____

_____

_____

_____

_____

_____

_____

_____

_____

_____

_____

_____

_____

_____

Chapter 8 Meditation Verse

No one has ever seen God, but the one and only Son,
who is himself God and is in closest relationship with him, he has made him known.

John 1:18

Day 1

_____

_____

_____

Day 2

_____

_____

_____

Day 3

_____

_____

_____

Day 4

_____

_____

_____

Day 5

_____

_____

_____

Chapter 8 Daily Prayer

Lord, help me to overcome the mindsets that position my heart to bear my pain.
Show me how to position my heart for healing.
Thank you, Lord, that I will experience healing by Your Spirit.

Write out anything you hear in your spirit or feel while you pray.

Day 1

_____

_____

_____

Day 2

_____

_____

_____

Day 3

_____

_____

_____

Day 4

_____

_____

_____

Day 5

_____

_____

_____

Things I'm Trusting God with This Week

_____

_____

_____

_____

_____

_____

_____

_____

_____

_____

_____

_____

_____

_____

_____

_____

_____

_____

_____

_____

_____

_____

Chapter 8: Identifying Self-Defeating Mindsets

Emotional healing is a process that is completed as God reveals truth to our hearts. When He reveals the truth to displace the lies we believe, the truth sets us free from the emotional turmoil those lies caused. Yet we may hear a truth a million times without the knowledge ever moving from our head, where we know it's true, to our heart, where we *feel* it's true. That's why emotional healing is so much more than head knowledge. When the Holy Spirit brings truth to our hearts by revelation, we finally understand what it means for us personally, and it changes the filters through which we see ourselves, God, and our circumstances.

Our role in the process of emotional healing is to simply ask and receive—that's all we can do. We cannot manipulate God's timing or convince Him to bend to our desires. There is no set of magic steps or a check-list to follow to receive the healing we need. However, one thing we can do to aid us on our journey is to recognize the mindsets, beliefs, and coping strategies we have that position our hearts to *bear our pain*. In confronting these mindsets, we can take intentional steps to change the position of our hearts from surviving to overcoming by His Spirit.

DENIAL

As discussed in Chapter 4, denying the truth of how we feel denies God the opportunity to heal us. We have to invite him into our reality rather than trying to convince him (and ourselves) that we live in a different reality altogether—one where we're not suffering, not hurting, not broken. We deny our feelings when we refuse to acknowledge them, or when we dismiss them without taking the time to properly process them. Denial can range from the overt, "I didn't let being sexually abused affect me," to an unconscious shifting of the thoughts away from anything that brings the sexual abuse experience and the resulting pain too close. Moving beyond denial to confession and invitation can be a difficult process, but it is perhaps the most necessary part of the healing journey. For a refresher on how to begin dealing with difficult emotions, see Chapter 4.

ACCEPTANCE

At the other end of the spectrum from denial is acceptance. Self-defeating acceptance happens when we accept the consequences of our abuse experience as facts of reality, rather than seeing them as wounds that can be healed. Acceptance can sound like, "I will always struggle with some parts of my past," or "Where I am now is better than where I used to be, so this is good enough."

Acceptance may present itself like wisdom and maturity, but it is actually a mask for fear and self-preservation: *If I don't hope for healing, I won't be disappointed when it doesn't happen. It's easier to be fine where I am than to pursue something painful that might not do any good.* We rarely stop to wonder if our mindsets line up with scripture. We tend to simply form judgments about what's possible based on what seems right to us.

SELF-CONDEMNATION

We practice self-condemnation any time we respond to our emotions with "should" or "shouldn't." *I should be over this by now. I shouldn't be struggling with this.* As I've shared before, this has long been my go-to response to negative emotional experiences. I don't initially allow myself to feel anxious or insecure, to feel disappointed or distressed, because I *should* know better. I should *be* better; I shouldn't be dealing with the same old thing again and again. Here's the thing, though: my beliefs about what I should or should not struggle with are irrelevant. They don't change the reality that I *do* struggle, period. The fact is that sometimes we struggle with fear, shame, insecurity, anger, or grief that stem from brokenness in our hearts. Shoulds and shouldn't *will not* and *cannot* change that.

It has taken years, but I've finally learned that resisting the hard work of actually processing my negative emotions only makes them last longer. As the saying goes, "What we resist persists." Processing our emotions is the only way through them; choosing not to process them, no matter how strongly we believe we shouldn't have to, only results in prolonged pain.

If you tend to condemn yourself for your emotional struggles, pray and ask the Lord to reveal the root cause of the condemnation. Often, it's shame, because we see our negative emotions as evidence of our failure and weakness. Just as often the root is pride, because deep down we believe we're better than that. Whatever He reveals, confess it and invite Him to do His work in your heart. Ask Him to help you see how *He* sees your struggles—what is His heart's response to your pain? Though your head might answer "grace, mercy, and love," your heart might not know for sure. Ask Him to bring healing through revelation of the truth.

FEAR

Fear is a powerful motivator, but instead of pushing us forward in the direction we need to go, it keeps us paralyzed right where we are. Fear leads us to deny, ignore, or dismiss the very feelings God is inviting us to feel so that He can heal them. We may fear the emotional pain we'll feel when we stop stuffing our emotions, or that redemption isn't a possibility for us. *Will I face my pain only to find I can't be healed? What if I'm too broken to be fixed? What if I open the door to this pain/anger/grief and get stuck there?*

As with acceptance, sometimes fear doesn't sound like fear at all. It sounds like wisdom or practicality: *I don't have time to fall apart right now. My family/job/church/ responsibilities need me.*

As you read in Chapter 6, "Redemption and Truth," I have spent huge parts of my journey absolutely paralyzed by fear: fear of judgment, fear of my own brokenness, fear that God's love wasn't real for me, fear that I was crazy to think the Lord was calling me to do anything (even if that something was a simple prayer with a friend—who did I think I was to believe I should pray with someone?). Even now, after immeasurable healing, if I step out in a new way, I always imagine other people are watching me, thinking, "*Who do you think you are?*"

Yet over time, the way the Lord and I deal with fear has changed. The pain-denial-brokenness-healing-repeat cycle morphed into the Holy Spirit's insistent reminder to acknowledge my motives: *am I making this decision to do or not do something out of fear?* If the answer is yes, His response is always the same: *act in the opposite spirit*. If fear says to do something, do the opposite, period.

I'll admit, I wasn't great at this at first. It took a while to grow from acknowledging my fear to acting in the opposite spirit, but then a seemingly small moment happened that somehow changed everything. I was prayer-journaling one morning when I found myself writing, "I'm tired of letting fear make my decisions, so this is it. No more." I've joked since then that the Lord tricked me into writing that—that I would no longer let fear make my decisions—because it didn't take long to realize it was a Spirit-led declaration. Within a year He had prompted me to publish my first book, *From Silence to Stories*, and begin my first sexual abuse recovery group, and those are only the "big" decisions. There have been lots of smaller choices to make along the way that fear would have made differently, but every time, the reminder was there: *Don't let fear make your decisions.*

Fear *can* be defeated. Its power *can* be broken. I doubt the day ever comes that fear no longer arises, but as our hearts are healed, the choice to act in the opposite spirit becomes easier. For now, begin renewing your mind by meditating and praying through scriptures that speak to fear. Ask the Lord to help you recognize when your motives are fear-based. Confess it and invite Him to lead you in courage and wisdom. Trust Him to show you what you need to do in each instance. Finally, talk everything through with a safe person and ask them to cover you in prayer and keep you accountable to obey the Lord's leading. Fear, like shame, is the most powerful when we keep it hidden, so take advantage of every opportunity to bring it into the light.

FALSE TEACHING

Certain teachings and popular sayings reinforce the idea that there is something wrong with us if we continue to struggle with our pasts. Others denote a false understanding of God's nature and His intervention in human affairs. For example:

"Depression and anxiety are faith issues."

The lie here is that depression and anxiety stem from a lack of faith. Some people believe that if you pray enough or read your Bible enough, you can overcome both.

The truth, however, is that mental illness, including depression and anxiety, are physiological issues that affect your brain chemistry. Yes, it is possible to combat the symptoms of either with the help of prayer, the Word, and the Holy Spirit. In fact, confession, prayer, and scripture meditation should always be your first response to anxiety and depression. Additionally, supernatural deliverance from both is possible. However, **depression and anxiety are not weaknesses to be ashamed of**; they are not choices a person makes. They are merely challenges some face, and they need to be regarded as such, without adding judgments against those who suffer.

"Everything happens for a reason."

As a philosophy, this one is exceptionally popular. People use it to explain away inexplicable tragedy, as if there is comfort in believing there's a reason for the terrible things that happen in the world.

From a Christian standpoint, however, the philosophy is wrong for a couple of reasons. For one, it does not line up with scripture. Proponents of this line of thinking may quote Romans 8:28, "And we know that in all things God works for the good of those who love him, who have been called according to his purpose." We must note, however, that the scripture does not say God causes everything to happen for some specific reason. Rather, it says He works everything that *does happen* for our good.

Secondly, rather than comforting someone who has experienced tragedy, this phrase is more likely to cause frustration and anger at God. The idea that there is some unidentifiable reason that supposedly makes a tragic loss or experience "worth it," and that God, therefore, has caused it, besmirches His character and heart for us.

"God is angry, frustrated, or disappointed with me."

Some denominations and religious traditions tend toward a legalistic worldview that espouses our need to "earn" God's favor, forgiveness, and love through good behavior. Again, this line of thinking is not true to God's character, nor does it align with scripture. As the Apostle Paul wrote to the church in Galatia, "I do not set aside the grace of God, for if righteousness [right standing with God] could be gained through [obedience to] the Law, then Christ died for nothing[22]." If you struggle with this mindset, ask the Holy Spirit to guide you through the Word and help you to see the truth of His grace in a new way.

"God will not give you more than you can handle."

As above, this idea is popular because it seems to line up with scripture. 1 Corinthians 10:13 says, "No temptation has overtaken you except what is common to mankind. And God is faithful; he will not let you be tempted beyond what you can bear. But when you are tempted, he will also provide a way out so that you can endure it." Some have taken the promise that God will not allow us to be tempted beyond what we can bear to mean nothing will happen to us that is more than we can handle.

The first problem with this loose interpretation is that the context of this verse is specific to temptation to sin, not general trials or tribulations. The second problem is that the idea that we should be able to handle everything in our lives on our own, without God's help, is itself contrary to scripture. For example, the Lord did not say to Joshua, "Be brave and courageous because you can totally handle this on your own." Instead, Joshua 1:9 says this: "Have I not commanded you? Be strong and courageous. Do not be afraid; do not be discouraged, for *the Lord your God will be with you wherever you go*." In other words, you will have reason to be afraid, reason to struggle, but He is with you, so you will never need to fear or struggle alone.

---

[22] Galatians 2:21

Like vows, judgments, and agreements, each of these beliefs must be confessed, rejected, and actively opposed.

FALSE UNDERSTANDING OF GOD'S NATURE

It's possible for us to love and serve God without truly knowing Him. We cannot, however, feel *secure* in Him if we don't truly know Him. We cannot rest in our place as His daughters if we misunderstand His character and nature. Until we know deep in our hearts who *He is*, we inevitably believe that who *we are* is what matters—leading us to strive and to earn rather than simply receive. Additionally, misunderstanding God's character can lead us to feel rejection, anger, disappointment, and frustration when God doesn't live up to our misguided expectations.

Some possible misunderstandings of God's nature include:

- The belief that God will (or should) reward us for obedient behavior. This can lead us to anger at God when we don't see the blessings or provision we feel we've earned, or to misinterpret situational struggles to mean God isn't happy with us.

- The belief that God is distant and angry. This can lead us to try to earn His approval with our good behavior, and in turn feel condemned and unloved when we inevitably fail.

- The belief that God gets annoyed with us or tired of providing for our constant needs. It can lead us to believe we should not pray about what we consider "small things" because He thinks we should be able to handle our lives on our own.

We can know and understand God's true nature by studying His son Jesus, who scripture says reveals the father to us. As John 1:18 says, "No one has ever seen God, but the one and only Son, who is himself God and is in closest relationship with him, he has made him known." If you read through the gospels paying special attention to how Jesus responds to people, you will gain a right understanding of God's love and compassion.

ADDICTION

Addiction is a coping strategy that keeps us from feeling our negative emotions or dealing with the painful memories of our pasts. We can develop addictions to anything: drugs/alcohol, sex, television, video games, or anything that allows us to control our environment and avoid our pain. We can even develop co-dependent tendencies that keep up focused on others rather than dealing with our own emotions. Some addictions seem harmless in comparison to others, but anything that prevents us from experiencing our true emotions and engaging with the Holy Spirit is detrimental to our healing journey and actually prolongs our pain.

Some addictions, such as those to drugs, sex, or alcohol may require counseling or recovery programs to overcome. Others can be overcome by learning new, healthy ways of coping with negative emotional experiences. Honestly assess your level of addiction and find a safe person with whom to discuss your needs. Never hesitate to seek out the professional help of a counselor or therapist as needed.

. . . .

Each of these mindsets help us cope with our negative emotions, but not in a healthy or productive way. In the next chapter we'll look at some spiritual disciplines we can develop to help us overcome our self-defeating tendencies.

Lord, thank You for not only revealing the mindsets and coping strategies that keep me bound to my pain, but also for freeing me from them. I ask that You continue helping me recognize these and any other self-defeating mindsets I have. I want to be completely free from every pattern of self-preservation that could hinder me from experiencing complete freedom and healing. Amen.

Chapter 8 Discussion

1. Ask the Lord to show you if there are any areas of struggle that you've accepted as inevitable. If something specific does or already has come to mind, write out a prayer of confession and invitation.

_____

_____

_____

_____

_____

_____

2. Look up Isaiah 43:2 in your favorite translation. Write it out as a prayer or declaration. For example, "When I walk through the fire, You are with me."

_____

_____

_____

_____

_____

3. Write out Joshua 1:9, Romans 8:38-39, or Isaiah 41:10. What does this verse mean to you?

_____

_____

_____

_____

_____

_____

_____

_____

_____

_____

_____

4. Have these or any other false teachings impacted your healing journey? Which ones? Take a moment to pray, rejecting each belief and breaking its power in your life in Jesus' name.

_____

_____

_____

_____

_____

5. Do you struggle with any addictive behaviors? Be real with yourself and God: confess your addictive behaviors and invite Him to free you from them. If you struggle with drug, alcohol, or sex addiction, declare your intention to seek help.

_____

_____

_____

_____

_____

6. Take a few moments to pray slowly through Psalm 139 from The Passion Translation.

[1] _Lord, you know everything there is to know about me._

2 You perceive every movement of my heart and soul, and you understand every thought before it enters my mind.

3-4 You are so intimately aware of me, Lord. You read my heart like an open book and you know all the words I'm about to speak before I even start a sentence! You know every step I will take before my journey even begins.

5 You have gone into my future to prepare the way, and in kindness you follow behind me to spare me from the harm of my past. With your hand of love upon my life, you impart blessing to me.

6 This is just too wonderful, deep, and incomprehensible! Your understanding of me brings me wonder and strength.

7 Where could I go from your Spirit? Where could I run and hide from your face?

8 If I go up to heaven, you're there! If I go down to the realm of the dead, you're there, too!

9 If I fly with wings into the shining dawn, you're there! If I fly into the radiant sunset, you're there waiting!

10 Wherever I go, your hand will guide me; your strength will empower me.

11 It's impossible to disappear from you or to ask the darkness to hide me, for your presence is everywhere bringing light into my night.

12 There is no such thing as darkness with you. The night, to you, is as bright as the day; there's no difference between the two.

13 You formed my innermost being, shaping my delicate inside and my intricate outside. and wove them all together in my mother's womb.

14 I thank you, God, for making me so mysteriously complex! Everything you do is marvelously breathtaking. It simply amazes me to think about! How thoroughly you know me, Lord!

15 You even formed every bone in my body when you created me in the secret place, carefully, skillfully shaping me from nothing to something.

16 You saw who you created me to be before I became me! Before I'd ever seen the light of day, the number of days you planned for me were already in your book.

17-18 Every single moment you are thinking of me! How precious and wonderful to consider that you cherish me constantly in your every thought! O God, your desires toward me are more than the grains of sand on every sea shore! When I awake each morning, you're still with me

[…]

23 God, I invite your searching gaze into my heart. Examine me through and through; find out everything that me be hidden within me. Put me to the test and sift through all my anxious cares.

24 See if there is any path of pain I'm walking on, and lead me back to your glorious ways – that path that brings me back to you.

7. What verses from the above psalm stuck out to you? Which promises mean the most to you at this moment? Write out your thoughts.

_____

_____

_____

_____

_____

_____

_____

_____

_____

_____

_____

_____

_____

_____

_____

_____

8. What other thoughts do you have about this chapter? What else is the Holy Spirit saying to you?

_____

_____

_____

_____

_____

_____

_____

_____

_____

_____

_____

_____

_____

_____

_____

_____

_____

_____

_____

Chapter 9 Meditation Verse

You desire but do not have, so you kill. You covet but you cannot get what you want, so you quarrel and fight. You do not have because you do not ask God.

James 4:2

Day 1

_____

_____

_____

Day 2

_____

_____

_____

Day 3

_____

_____

_____

Day 4

_____

_____

_____

Day 5

_____

_____

_____

Chapter 9 Daily Prayer

Lord, I pray that you would strengthen me through
Your spirit in my inner being.
May I be rooted and established in Your love so that
Your love is the foundation my life is built on.
I pray You would help me to understand the fullness of
Your love—its length, width, height, and depth.
Help me to know Your love that passes natural understanding, so that
I can live at maximum capacity, filled to the measure with the fullness of God.

Write out anything you hear in your spirit or feel while you pray.

Day 1

_____

_____

_____

Day 2

_____

_____

_____

Day 3

_____

_____

_____

Day 4

_____

_____

_____

Day 5

_____

_____

_____

Things I'm Trusting God with This Week

_____

_____

_____

_____

_____

_____

_____

_____

_____

_____

_____

_____

_____

_____

_____

_____

_____

Chapter 9: Developing Spiritual Disciplines

Identifying the self-defeating mindsets, beliefs, and coping strategies that position our hearts to bear our pain rather than pursue the Lord for healing is a vital step toward positioning our hearts to receive all that God has for us. The next step is to intentionally develop disciplines that help us get free from those mindsets and stay free from them. Some of these disciplines, such as prayer and taking our thoughts captive, will be familiar, but do not allow familiarity or your preconceived notions about what each discipline must look like to influence your attitude toward them. Pray and ask the Lord to help you see each discipline with fresh eyes.

Additionally, the idea of "disciplines" can sometimes trigger feelings of fear, inadequacy, and failure. However, the purpose of this chapter is not to shame you, but to empower you, to show you how to take familiar "tools" and utilize them on your healing journey. They are not necessary to "please" God—He's already pleased with you—and they are not intended to become a part of your checklist. As you read through this chapter, pay special attention to your thoughts and attitude toward each discipline, and confess any negative responses to the Lord as you go along.

Take a moment now to invite the Lord to help you see these disciplines with new eyes. Write out your prayer in the space provided on the following page.

THE DISCIPLINE OF PRAYER

Prayer is one thing we all know we should do, but most of us don't actually utilize to its full potential. Because prayer feels so much like a "should," we tend to get overwhelmed or intimidated by our inability to pray "enough." I'm not here to add to that feeling. Instead I want to encourage you with some principles of prayer that invite us into a deeper relationship with God.

The first is found in a familiar scripture, James 4:2. It says, "You desire but do not have, so you kill. You covet but you cannot get what you want, so you quarrel and fight. You do not have because you do not ask God."

For years I would read this verse and not think past the literal and material. "Kill" and "quarrel and fight" are such strong words that they're hard to relate to our everyday experience. But when reading this verse in the context of sexual abuse recovery, I think about what we as survivors desire and the ways in which we go about trying to fulfill those desires.

For example, we want to feel valued and loved, but sexual abuse often leaves survivors believing they're only valuable for their sexual contributions to a relationship, so that's what we use to satisfy our longing. We don't recognize the deeper need, so we seek to fill it the only way we know: through sexual and emotional promiscuity.

However, God has chosen prayer as His means of provision. James 4:2 says, "You do not have because you do not ask God." We know He wants to provide for us the things we desire, but He also allows us to search for those things wherever we choose. He wants us to choose to seek Him. Sometimes even that is a process, but that process will always begin one way: with prayer.

Seeking God in prayer is an essential part of any kind of recovery. As mentioned in previous chapters, nothing can take the place of your participation in your healing journey through prayer. More than anything else we might do, prayer positions our hearts to hear from the Lord. When we pour out our hearts like water in His presence[23], He can then refill us with His truth and His love.

In order to get the full benefit of an active prayer life, we must remember that prayer is about more than listing our needs; it's about more than getting our prayers "answered." Prayer is about communion with God. When we commune with God, we *exchange* intimate thoughts and feelings. We give Him ours, and He gives us His. That's why you are encouraged to regularly pray prayers of confession and invitation. Confess to Him your intimate thoughts and feelings and invite Him to speak His truth to your heart.

> Communion: the exchanging of intimate thoughts and feelings

The spirit is willing…

Prayer is also God's means for filling us with courage and stamina for the battles ahead. In each of the gospels, we see Jesus' final act before His arrest: He went to the garden to pray. He knew His arrest was imminent; He knew He was at that very moment being betrayed by Judas Iscariot and would soon be abandoned by each of His disciples. The Bible tells us in Mark 14:34 that when He arrived at the Garden of Gethsemane, He was deeply troubled, distressed to the point of death. He took the three disciples He was closest to, went farther into the garden away from the others, and asked the three to watch and pray. Then He went farther along until He was alone, fell on His knees, and sought His Father in prayer. We don't know how long He prayed, only that He prayed for God to remove the cup from Him—yet not His will, but God's will be done. When He went back to His three closest friends—the ones He had told again and again what was coming, the ones He had asked specifically to watch for the coming horde and to pray they wouldn't fall into temptation—they were sleeping.

---

[23] Lamentations 2:19

Two more times Jesus asked them to watch and pray, then went away to pray alone, and every time He came back to find them sleeping. Finally, Judas arrived with a crowd to arrest Jesus, and He, the one whose soul had been distressed to the point of death, the one who had been so distressed His sweat was like drops of blood, the one who had sought His Father's presence in prayer—He was perfectly calm.

...but the flesh is weak.

His disciples, on the other hand, completely lost it. Peter drew his sword and cut off a soldier's ear, then they all panicked and ran away, leaving Jesus to face His fate alone.

The lesson we learn from this can be easily summed up: pray and stay or run away. As you already know, your journey to emotional healing is not a happy stroll on a sunlit beach. There are moments of that—moments of sweet peace and victory, moments of rest—but then it's back to the garden where you're tired, scared, and overwhelmed. You'll be faced with countless opportunities to choose: stay and pray or run away. Stay in the garden, pressing into the Lord, seeking Him and drawing from His strength. Or run away, back to your coping strategies and defense mechanisms, back to the habits and addictions that numb the pain.

The spirit is willing to be healed. The spirit is willing to fight the hard fight to overcome every last blow of the enemy. But the flesh is weak. Our flesh will do anything to avoid the fight. The only way to fight the temptation to run away and hide from our pain is to watch and pray.

Philippians 4:6-7 (NLT) says this:

> *"Don't worry about anything; instead, pray about everything.*
> *Tell God what you need and thank him for all he has done.*
> *Then you will experience God's peace,*
> *which exceeds anything we can understand.*
> *His peace will guard your hearts and minds*
> *as you live in Christ Jesus."*

Others can pray for us all day long, but the peace that passes understanding comes when *we* submit our needs to God. In His grace He may grant you the peace others pray for you to have, but it's only a temporary bandage to get you through a tough moment. What each of us needs is peace that *guards our hearts and minds* as we continue our journey. According to scripture, that peace is a direct result of us submitting our needs to God in prayer.

Beginning a regular prayer life may mean taking baby-steps, and that's okay.

- Don't pressure yourself. Remember that you are not trying to earn God's grace and favor through prayer. The purpose of prayer is not to manipulate God's heart, but to position *your* heart to receive all that He has for you.

- Don't set yourself up for failure by creating unreasonable goals. Don't be ashamed to start small. One good method is to put on a playlist of your favorite worship songs, then pray and worship through one or more songs. If it's easier to pray when you're doing something, you can pray in the car on your way to work, as you do the dishes, or through any other routine activity. Using a prayer journal to write out your prayers and anything the Lord speaks to your heart while you pray will provide you with a record of your victories, reminding you of how far you've come when you're tempted to feel hopeless about how far you have to go.

- Don't 'should' yourself: *I should pray longer. I should pray better. I should sound more spiritual.* Remember, you're not trying to earn God's grace and favor through prayer. (Redundant, I know, but important enough to say twice.) You can just be yourself before God and trust Him to guide you.

THE DISCIPLINE OF TAKING OUR THOUGHTS CAPTIVE

2 Corinthians 10:5 is another familiar verse:

> *We demolish arguments and every pretension*
> *that sets itself up against the knowledge of God,*
> *and we take captive every thought*
> *to make it obedient to Christ.*

You might be familiar with this scripture and the concept of taking your thoughts captive, but, if you're like most of us, you're not always great at applying it. In the context of emotional healing, taking our thoughts captive means recognizing when our thoughts and feelings don't line up with the truth, and then rejecting them intentionally. This is as simple and practical as saying out loud, "I reject the lie that _____." Or, "I reject the shame I feel about _____." Doing so does not result in an immediate change of heart and mind, but it is the first step to bringing our minds and hearts into alignment with God's truth. In order to get free from self-defeating thought habits, we have to acknowledge and reject our wrong thinking through confession and invite the Lord to help us know the truth.

The hardest part of the process is recognizing the lies as we think them. We've often spent years either dismissing/denying our thoughts and feelings related to our abuse experience, or else indulging them as though they're true. As you have walked through this material, you've probably already begun taking your thoughts captive, so this isn't new information. It's just a reminder to prioritize this discipline. Ask the Lord to help you grow in recognizing every argument and "every pretension that sets itself up against the knowledge of God." Invite Him to replace the lies with the truth.

THE DISIPLINE OF RENEWING YOUR MIND

Romans 12:2 tells us,

> *Do not conform to the pattern of this world,*
> *but be transformed by the renewing of your mind.*
> *Then you will be able to test and approve what God's will is—*
> *His good, pleasing, and perfect will.*

Our minds are renewed by spending time in the Word. We know that the Word of God is the only way to understand His truth. Through it we learn the character and nature of God, as well as learning how to live in the fullness of His love and purpose for our lives. The Bible is essential for that, because it's far too easy to form beliefs and opinions that are contrary to His heart.

If you're not already spending time in the Word four or five days a week, I encourage you to start. You probably shouldn't open your Bible to Genesis 1, though you can. A better place to start is with one of the Gospels or an epistle like Philippians or Ephesians.

> "Your word is a lamp to guide my feet and a light for my path."
>
> Psalm 199:105 (NLT)

As with each of these disciplines, don't be afraid to start small. Even if you begin by only reading half a chapter a day—even if you only spend a few minutes meditating on a Bible app's verse of the day—that's a good place to start. Remember, you're not reading your Bible to please God, to look good, or to earn something. You are reading it in order to renew your mind, to soak up God's truth, and to get to know Him better.

THE DISCIPLINE OF VULNERABILITY

Vulnerability is the "state of being exposed to the possibility of being attacked or harmed, either physically or emotionally." Of course, in the context of emotional healing, "attacked or harmed" is subjective. Rather than using God's truth to determine what will harm us, our pain, fear, and shame usually decides, and those things are inevitably wrong. To find freedom from our pain we have to feel it, but everything in us pushes us to do the exact opposite: deny it, dismiss it, hide it.

The good news is that God is a safe place for us to feel our feelings. God is love[24]. That means He is patient, kind, gentle, gracious, and merciful[25]. He is kind even to the ungrateful and wicked[26], so no matter what you've done, no matter how you may have flouted His goodness to you, He will never respond to you in anger. He is a safe place to be vulnerable.

More good news: God created the Body of Christ to be His representatives in the

---

[24] 1 John 4:8

[25] 1 Corinthians 13:4-7

[26] Luke:35

God is patient and kind. He does not envy, does not boast, and is not proud. He will not dishonor you. He will not seek only His own pleasure at your expense. He is not easily angered, and He keeps no record of wrongs. He does not delight in harm, but He rejoices in the truth.

flesh. It's easy to believe that we "should" be able to get healing through communion with God alone—and I would be the last to say you can't—but I also know that God gave us the analogy of the body for a reason[27]. He has designed us to need each other, to draw from each other. He has placed in each of us gifts and insight that we are to use to minister His love and healing to others.

You do not have to be vulnerable with everyone, or even more than one, but you do need at least one person that you can be completely real and honest with, someone with whom you can share your deepest thoughts and feelings. Every one of us needs someone who will allow us to express the depth of our feelings without trying to talk us out of feeling that way, even if what we feel isn't rational or sensible. We need to be allowed and encouraged to express the truth of our emotions.

If something in you resists the idea of vulnerability with the Body of Christ or with God, first you must acknowledge the root of your resistance, which is most likely pain, fear, or shame. Discovering or acknowledging the root can be a difficult process, but it is a vital step to freedom. Next, reject the pain, fear, shame, etc., out loud, and ask God to speak truth to the lies that led to your resistance.

Finally, begin acting in the opposite spirit by cultivating vulnerability even in the smallest way. Again, don't be ashamed to start small.

THE DISCIPLINE OF SPIRITUAL REST

The discipline of rest comes in two parts: spiritual and natural rest. Spiritual rest is resting in God's plan, purpose, and heart toward you. We rest spiritually when we know that God is in control of our circumstances no matter how out-of-control

---

[27] 1 Corinthians 12:12-27

they seem; when we know that we are perfectly secure in His love, not needing to work or earn our place in His heart; and when we know that He is our Provider for everything we need, regardless of the lack we perceive in our circumstances. It's more than head knowledge, which does nothing to calm our souls. Rest requires *heart knowledge*, knowledge we not only know but feel, knowledge that silences the lies of the enemy and our own insecurities.

It's probably easy to see why rest is a discipline. Psalm 46:10 (NASB) exhorts us this way:

> *Cease striving and know that I am God.*
> *I will be exalted among the nations,*
> *I will be exalted in the earth!*

But striving is our default. We strive to please, strive to earn, strive to keep it together, or at the very least, to *look* like we're keeping it together. As women—moms, wives, bosses, employees, volunteers—we strive to do our best, to serve, to help, to nurture, to support. Striving is what we do best.

Rest, on the other hand, means accepting ourselves and our situations for what they are, without anger at God or judgment against ourselves, yet with hope for redemption and healing. Rest means trusting that we have God's love and favor simply because we're His daughters. And rest means being okay with not being okay, even when it is both embarrassing for ourselves and inconvenient for the ones we love.

Spiritual rest is trust in action.

Contrary to what rest sounds like, spiritual rest requires us to work hard to take our thoughts captive and to renew our minds to the truth, to refuse to conform to the patterns of this world or even to the patterns we see in church culture. Rest is a daily, hourly, even minute-ly decision that we will often forget we have to make. But as we take our thoughts captive, as we spend time in the Word and in prayer, as we grow in intimacy with God, we *will* learn to rest in Him. Resting in Him will become easier and easier; we will learn to revert to resting rather than striving more quickly, though we will probably never "arrive" as perfect resters. When we come to a season through which we must grow in trust in order to experience healing, we will grow in rest at the same time.

THE DISCIPLINE OF NATURAL REST

The second aspect of rest is natural rest, when we embrace seasons of resting our hearts, minds, bodies, and emotions. You probably don't need someone to tell you that an overwhelmed, exhausted you is not the best you—not for your family, not for the Body of Christ, and not for your own emotional health. In order to function at the height of our potential, we have to take care of ourselves—again, even if it's inconvenient to those around us.

Of course, knowing that rest is necessary doesn't stop us from going and going until we're ready to fall apart. Busy, capable, high-functioning women tend to think of self-care as something "weak" women do. We rarely stop to consider that self-care is something obedient women do, per the proverb:

> *Guard your heart above all else, for it is the source of life.*

> Proverbs 4:23

In popular Christian culture, this verse is usually used to refer to dating and romantic relationships, as though our hearts are only good for falling in love. According to scripture, however, our hearts are responsible for much more.

Our hearts determine:

- How generous we are—with everything, not just money (2 Corinthians 9:7)—

  Each person should do as he has decided in his heart—
  not reluctantly or out of necessity, for God loves a cheerful giver.

- The words we speak (Luke 6:45)—

  A good man produces good out of the good storeroom of his heart.
  An evil man produces evil out of the evil storeroom,
  for his mouth speaks from the overflow of the heart.

- The sins we choose (Mark 7:21-22)—

  *For from within, out of people's hearts, come evil thoughts,
  sexual immorality, thefts, murders, adulteries, greed, evil actions,
  deceit, promiscuity, stinginess, blasphemy, pride, and foolishness.*

- Our plans (Proverbs 16:9)—

  A man's heart plans his way, but the Lord determines his steps.

- Our desires (Psalm 37:4)—

  Take delight in the Lord, and he will give you the desires of your heart.

Our hearts also reflect who we are (Proverbs 27:19)—

  As water reflects the face, so the heart reflects the person.

It's easy to see, then, why we need to guard our hearts diligently. Though we can follow the command in several different ways, none of them is more vitally important to our spiritual and emotional health than rest. A frantic, frazzled, exhausted heart is an open door to the enemy, like issuing an invitation to torment us with *more* duty, *more* unrealistic expectations, and *more* failure. The more exhausted we are, the harder time we have discerning what is good and true and what is harmful, whether in our schedule, our self-talk, or our perception of God.

How we rest is determined by how God created us. What is restful for one might not be restful for someone else, so the important thing is not how you rest, but just that you rest.

Even though it's hard—

Even though it's inconvenient—

Even though you've spent years doing the exact opposite—

Begin making time regularly to rest, whatever that looks like for you.

You could:

- engage in a creative activity like art journaling or crafting

- tend a garden

- read for pleasure

- binge-watch your favorite show

- exercise

- have coffee with a friend

One more thing: rest is not only an activity, but also a state of mind. If you struggle with feeling obligated to serve others, care for them, or be a certain type of person to the detriment of your own emotional health, take those thoughts and feelings to the Lord. Confess the insecurities that keep you busy beyond what is good for you and invite Him to speak truth and healing to your heart. Ask Him to help you become a person who guards their heart with rest.

. . . .

Each of the spiritual disciplines outlined in this chapter help us position our hearts to experience emotional healing. Our old mindsets, defense mechanisms, and thought patterns may have allowed us to cope with our spiritual and emotional issues, but they do not contribute to healing. These spiritual disciplines, however, *do* contribute to the healing process by changing the way we perceive ourselves, God, and our circumstances. Intimate prayer, taking our thoughts captive, renewing our minds with the Word, practicing vulnerability, and spiritual and natural rest are all disciplines that will lead to better spiritual and emotional health in every area of our lives. They are worth the time and effort required to develop them.

Lord, I ask for Your help and leading as I develop these spiritual disciplines. May I be led by Your Spirit—not by shame, legalism, or a misguided desire to please you. Help me to know which of these disciplines to focus on first, and I ask You to help me remember to rest any time I begin to feel overwhelmed or insufficient. **Amen.**

Chapter 9 Discussion

1. Assess your current prayer life. Do you have the intimacy with the Lord that you want and that He wants with you? If not, what is keeping you from it?

_____

_____

_____

_____

_____

_____

2. What baby-steps can you take to begin a discipline of prayer?

_____

_____

_____

_____

_____

3. Write out a prayer asking the Lord to help you take your thoughts captive. If there are any negative or destructive thought patterns you struggle with, write them down and invite the Lord's intervention.

_____

_____

_____

_____

_____

_____

4. Review the discipline of renewing your mind. What scripture has the Lord used at a specific time to renew your mind to His truth? Write it out.

_____

_____

_____

_____

_____

_____

5. What happens in your heart when you think of making yourself vulnerable through sharing your deepest heart with God or others? For example, do you feel anxious? Afraid? Peaceful?

_____

_____

_____

_____

_____

_____

6. Which activity of our hearts described on page 151 stood out to you the most? Explain why.

_____

_____

_____

_____

_____

_____

7. Consider the phrase, "Rest is trust in action." What does that mean to you?

_____

_____

_____

_____

_____

8. Is spiritual rest difficult for you? What are some steps you could take to begin resting in the Lord?

_____

_____

_____

_____

_____

9. Do you resist natural rest? Do you find it difficult to engage in self-care? Write out your thoughts.

_____

_____

_____

_____

_____

10. What other thoughts do you have about this chapter? What else is the Holy Spirit saying to you?

_____

_____

_____

_____

_____

_____

_____

_____

_____

_____

_____

_____

_____

_____

_____

_____

_____

_____

_____

_____

_____

_____

_____

Chapter 10 Meditation Verse

Create in me a pure heart, O God, and renew a steadfast spirit within me.

Psalm 51:10

Day 1

_____

_____

_____

Day 2

_____

_____

_____

Day 3

_____

_____

_____

Day 4

_____

_____

_____

Day 5

_____

_____

_____

Chapter 10 Daily Prayer

Lord, help me to forgive the ones who abused me, wounded my heart, and failed to protect me. Show me what true freedom through forgiveness and healing can look like and strengthen my heart to pursue it.

Write out anything you hear in your spirit or feel while you pray.

Day 1

_____

_____

_____

Day 2

_____

_____

_____

Day 3

_____

_____

_____

Day 4

_____

_____

_____

Day 5

_____

_____

_____

Things I'm Trusting God with This Week

_____

_____

_____

_____

_____

_____

_____

_____

_____

_____

_____

_____

_____

_____

_____

_____

_____

_____

_____

_____

_____

_____

Chapter 10: Forgiveness and Healing

Forgiveness can be a tricky subject for trauma survivors. Cognitively, we know we are commanded to forgive others just as God forgives us. Jesus Himself said, "For if you forgive other people when they sin against you, your heavenly Father will also forgive you. But if you do not forgive others their sins, your Father will not forgive your sins[28]."

It's hard to argue with that, right? Forgiveness is a choice we have to make, period.

Sometimes, however, for a million different reasons, our mind and emotions resist the command to forgive. We can easily become overwhelmed by the responsibility of forgiveness as we slog through the real-life emotions of trauma, and we may forget that the choice to forgive is merely the first step in a potentially long and difficult process. If we say, "I forgive that person" over and over without ever seeing any change in how we feel, we may become discouraged, or worse, we may accept that forgiveness with continued pain is as good as it gets.

We settle for what our experience says is true, never stopping to question whether or not "this is it."

In fact, when it comes to discussing or thinking about forgiveness, we rarely get past the "what it is/what it isn't" stage: "Forgiveness doesn't mean you trust them; forgiveness doesn't mean you restore the relationship." These statements are true and valid, but they barely scratch the surface of what forgiveness is, and they seem to reveal a

---

[28] Matthew 6:14-15

defensive stance, as though we're so concerned with protecting our hearts from what forgiveness might require of us that we miss the opportunity for the grace of God to work it out in us.

That's why, for this discussion, I don't want to rehash the "what forgiveness is and isn't" conversation (though, for the sake of clarity, more on this topic can be found on page 171). Instead, I want to talk about hope, about healing and freedom, about a deep-down work that can unlock parts of our hearts that we assumed would be barred shut forever.

Forgiveness is about hope, healing, and freedom. The reality of forgiveness is so much more than we imagine—so much richer, so much more joyful. This chapter is about what it can look and feel like when we allow the Lord to work it out in us by His Spirit, when we choose to trust Him with our deepest hurts, our most painful wounds, our fiercest anger.

He is able to do exceedingly, abundantly more in our hearts than we could ever ask or imagine by His Spirit at work within us, and that includes leading us to complete, *heartfelt* forgiveness.

I have to admit, before this project I had only shared my own story of forgiveness toward my abuser once or maybe twice, and even then, only with close friends. I have always seen my story as too strangely personal to be helpful to others. But then, in the week leading up to the forgiveness discussion in my very first recovery group, the Lord showed me otherwise. It all began with an antique book I'd picked up at a church garage sale several months before titled *The Calling of Dan Matthews*. I had purchased the book for several reasons, not the least of which was that Dan Mathews is my dad's name. I was curious to see how I'd feel reading a book with his name prominently displayed on every page. When I got the book home, however, I put it on my shelf and left it. Every day it would catch my eye, but I resisted picking it up. When I finally forced myself to start it the first time, I read a few pages, but began to feel panicky the closer it got to the character of Dan being introduced. I put it down and told the Lord I had no idea why I felt that sudden and uncharacteristic rush of heart-pounding anxiety, and, because I didn't like the idea of being bothered by something as innocuous as my dad's name in a book, I asked Him to fix it.

Judging by the way it all worked out, I now think that rush of what I call anxiety was the Holy Spirit intervening because it wasn't time for me to read it yet. The Lord had plans in mind, and I was rushing them.

I don't remember what made me pick it up again a few months later, but when I did, the anxiety was gone. It took me a couple of weeks—books published in 1909 are not known for being gripping page-turners—but I when finished it on a Sunday morning before church—significantly, just a few days before my recovery group's discussion on forgiveness—I found myself feeling things I didn't know what to do with. I had enjoyed the book very much; not only is the story pretty good, but the character of Dan Matthews is an interesting man. He has lots of admirable qualities and some intriguing flaws. He was not the perfect, selfless hero often seen in that era's literature. However, none of that seemed to explain the thought that plagued me all morning, one I couldn't shake: *My dad was a good man.*

Just thinking that thought opened the door for all kinds of arguments, because, obviously, my dad was not anyone's definition of a good man. He was a child molester and rapist. How could he also be a good man? The idea didn't make sense. I kept trying to formulate how I would say the words out loud to another person—"My dad was a good man"—but I couldn't get past how ridiculous they sounded. How could I argue that the man who sexually abused me was good in any way?

Yet I kept remembering little things about my dad that brought up unexpected joy: a silly smile he would give us that I still see on my twin brother's face when he's being sweet; the way Dad would tap out the beat to music on the radio with specific fingers, as though he were playing the song on his bass guitar. And no matter how rational my arguments sounded, I couldn't shake the idea that my dad *had been* a good man.

Since it was a Sunday morning, I was able to put the argument aside to some degree and focus on our pre-church routine. It wasn't until the praise and worship part of the church service that I finally prayed about it. I simply asked, "Lord, what's all this for?"

Forgiveness is not only a command. It is a conduit of God's mercy toward us.

Did I expect an answer? To be honest, probably not, but it came just the same, as clearly as if He had spoken it out loud.

One word: forgiveness.

Lots of ideas came together in that moment, all focused on how I would approach the recovery group's discussion that week. The Lord told me clearly to tell my weird, never-heard-anything-like-it-before story, not to "teach" my ladies to forgive, but to offer hope for what forgiveness can do in their hearts.

My story:

As a quick recap, my dad began molesting me when I was around nine years old. Over the next six months or so, it progressed from molestation to rape, and continued until just a few months before my twelfth birthday, when I told a friend at school what was happening. My dad was arrested in April of that year. Despite his confession, he refused to plead guilty to the charges, so in September of that year, I testified at the preliminary hearing and then in March I testified at his jury trial. (I would love to speculate on why he refused to plead guilty despite having admitted to the abuse—did he think I'd recant? Did he truly believe he hadn't done anything wrong?—but that's a judgment I can't make.) He was sentenced to 420 years in prison, plus life. A few months later he was murdered.

I was too young and confused at the time of his death to understand the lifelong impact of what my dad had done. I definitely didn't know that the rest of my life would be defined by sexual abuse in some way or another. I only knew that my dad, who had always been kind and loving to me, was dead. I had never been angry with him. Had certainly never hated him. I'm sure at some point I would have felt that anger as I grew up and became more aware of the damage he had done, if not for one event.

A few days after my dad's death, my mom told me of a vision she'd had of dad on the night he'd died. She'd been sitting alone in the living room, thinking and praying, when she saw him in her mind. First, he was bound up in heavy chains, tormented, sick, and hopeless. Then the chains began to break and fall until he was free. She said she knew right away what it meant: while alive, he had been bound up in chains, spiritually and emotionally imprisoned by the sin that had come to control him. At the moment of his death, his spirit was restored, set free.

I think if there was ever a moment of forgiveness for me toward him, it was then. Somehow that picture of him bound up by sin and deception—even though it was long before I had the emotional or spiritual maturity to understand what that meant—set me free from the lie that *I* had anything to do with his choices. His own sickness caused him to do what he did. The lie that I might have somehow contributed to it through my own actions or sexual curiosity was broken before it ever had a chance to take root.

As I prayed and journaled my way through this story that day after finishing *The Calling of Dan Matthews*, two thoughts came to mind.

Forgiveness and Judgment

Forgiveness brings freedom to our hearts because holding on to judgment about another person's value based on their actions—no matter how reprehensible those actions were—is like opening the door to the enemy of our souls and inviting him in to torment us. Like any other judgment or agreement with the enemy, unforgiveness will seep into my heart and color my view of everyone, myself included. I will soon become unable to differentiate between people and their actions, causing me to see everyone—again, myself included—as sinners, rather than as sons and daughters of the Most High. Refusing to extend forgiveness will inevitably lead to an inability to forgive myself; rather than recognizing the Lord's grace and mercy toward me, I will feel only shame and condemnation for my mistakes.

We know this already, but I have to say it because it's true: Forgiveness isn't about the other person. It's about us—our own healing, our own freedom. We've all heard it said that unforgiveness is like drinking poison and expecting the other person to die. I'll say it a little differently (and less concisely): holding steadfastly to our judgments of another person's worth and value based on what they've done and our opinions about what they deserve is like blinding ourselves and expecting the other person to suffer. Those judgments and opinions become the filter through which we see the entire world; they determine what we see in ourselves, God, and others. We can hinder ourselves from fully accepting the truth of God's mercy and forgiveness in our own lives. Unforgiveness and judgment open the door to the enemy to torment us with condemnation for our own failures. Judgment against others can prevent me from receiving the truth of God's love into the deepest parts of my heart where I need it most.

Forgiveness and Emotional Healing

The combined result of forgiveness and emotional healing is that we no longer feel the need to protect ourselves. Forgiving my dad allowed me to see him as a whole person, to allow the good to stand on its own, unaffected by the bad. I believe I was able to do that so early and so easily because I no longer had to protect myself from him, both in the literal sense because he went to prison and soon died, and in the figurative sense, because the power of the lie that would have shaped my identity was broken. From the moment my mom told me about her vision, I no longer had to protect my heart from the lie that what he did was my fault. The power that he and his actions would have had to continue wreaking destruction in my life was broken completely. Though I still had a lot of years of dealing with the consequences of the abuse itself, said consequences were no longer connected to him as the perpetrator. Anger, betrayal, a deep sense of rejection at being so easily misused by my own father—the destructive power of those factors was broken before it had a chance to take root.

Forgiving my mom, on the other hand, was a totally different story. Her propensity to use verbal insults, fault-finding, and irrational criticism to control those around her remains the same. Her words continued to hurt and anger me for years, and they would still be eliciting hurt and anger, except that over time the Lord healed my heart of the wounds she created and perpetuated in my identity. He led me to release her from all expectation, so that I could stop looking to her to be the mom I wanted and needed and accept that she would only ever be who she is unless and until the Lord intervenes.

Only after that was I able to see her as a whole person, and to let her be herself without taking it personally. I don't have to protect my heart from her anymore because her words no longer have the power to hurt me. When the Lord healed my identity, He showed me that her words and actions have nothing to do with me. They're not about me; I don't deserve them; they don't accurately represent who I am. When those lies were displaced, forgiveness was natural and even easy.

Those two separate experiences show me that forgiveness and emotional healing are divinely connected. I can't experience complete forgiveness without emotional healing, but I also can't have emotional healing without being willing to forgive. Even the first fledgling steps of forgiveness require submission to God's authority as my protector. I had to be willing to stop protecting myself from my mom with my own anger and allow Him to protect my heart with the truth.

Forgiveness and Self-Preservation

When we resist walking out the process of forgiveness for our abusers or the ones who failed to protect us, we don't do so out of anger—though it can look like anger. We don't resist out of judgment or vengeance, though it can look like both. All of those things are actually masks for self-preservation. For example, I've prayed with a sister who had refused to forgive her children's abuser because she feared that letting go of her anger would mean she wouldn't have the strength or will to pursue justice for her daughters. In her mind, forgiveness meant letting him off the hook, something she could not do for her daughters' sake. She was using her anger to protect herself and her children, rather than allowing God to be her protector. And though she was relying on her anger to literally be her children's protector, we do the same thing emotionally and spiritually. We use anger and judgment to protect our hearts from the lies that tell us who we are because of our abuse experience.

Emotional healing comes by His Spirit, not by our own will. The only thing we have to do is be willing to surrender to Him (to surrender means *to cease resistance)*;

> **The work of forgiveness is completed by His Spirit.**

we have to choose to be protected rather than being our own protector. We must submit to God every area where we feel the need to protect ourselves and ask Him to help us trust Him to be our protector. We need to ask Him, "What wound needs to be healed so that I can trust You to protect my heart? What lie needs to be displaced?"

A word about guilt:

Any time I share about my dad's death, I get asked the same question: "Did you feel guilty for what happened to him?" My answer seems to come as a surprise, because I have always said no, I never felt guilty. I knew even as a teenager that my dad went to prison for breaking the law. Him being there when he died was not my fault but was instead a direct result of the choices he made. I had no reason to feel guilt, so I didn't.

And up until a short time ago, I still believed that was true.

Feeling guilt for things that happened to us is our way of taking responsibility for them. We shoulder the responsibility for the consequences of someone else's actions or choices, and thanks to the power of emotional deception, our hearts feel like it truly is ours to carry, even when our rational minds tell us otherwise.

Recently, I've realized that feeling guilty is not the only way to shoulder that responsibility. I may have never felt guilt in the traditional sense, but I did feel responsible. See, I'd always loved my dad tremendously. Between my two parents, he was the "nice" one. There was a lot of verbal, emotional, and physical abuse in our household coming from our mom, but our dad rarely got angry, rarely yelled, never said mean or cruel things. He was overly permissive, letting me get away with anything I wanted, but I was too young to see that for the grooming technique it was. He was a good dad in my eyes, and that didn't change when he began molesting me. I quickly learned how to dissociate my daytime hours from the nighttime ones; I simply didn't think about the sexual abuse during the day. It was almost like I forgot it completely. Since my mom was the one who was physically and emotionally abusive, she was the one I wanted to get away from—so badly that I even told my dad I wanted to live with him.

I can see now many different layers of trauma and deception were informing my thoughts and actions. My dad was the one who made me feel loved. He was the one who was kind and affectionate. My mom was the one who made me feel small and stupid, who told me I was that and more on a regular basis. So, my young-girl's heart latched onto the love with both hands and didn't let go. My dad loved me, and I felt I needed to protect that love—to earn it, to keep it, because I wasn't getting it from anyone else. I had decided I was never going to tell anyone about the sexual abuse because I didn't want anything bad to happen to him. I didn't want to lose him and the love he represented.

Telling my friend at school that day was a choice I instantly regretted. Suddenly I was being swept along a path that twisted every second between relief and terror. I began to love my dad even more than I already had, because somewhere the lie came in that I could protect him with my love. As long as I loved him, he would be safe. But more importantly, as long as I loved him, he would still love me.

Obviously, it wasn't true that my love could keep him safe. But the feeling that I could love him into loving me never went away; even after he was dead, it persisted, and then I applied it to my relationship with God. When my husband and I began attending church and serving the Lord with our daily lives, I jumped into my relationship with Him with a frantic need to earn His love. If I served Him tirelessly, prayed and read the Word relentlessly, and felt unmatched affection for Him, then His love would be secured. I subconsciously believed I had to convince Him to love me through devotion and attention. This was the first lie the Lord ever revealed to me. Before that, I didn't know it was even possible to have beliefs about God that weren't true. It took several years for my heart to fully know and feel the truth that I am secure in His love no matter what.

So, no, I never felt guilty for my dad's death, but I did take on the responsibility for the consequences of his choices in a way that shaped my thoughts and actions for years to come. When the Lord healed my heart of the lies that caused me to take on that responsibility, I was essentially forgiving myself for the role I had subconsciously believed I played in my dad's death.

· ·

Saying the words "I forgive this person" is merely the first step in a potentially long and difficult process, but it is a vitally important step. Because forgiveness and emotional healing are divinely connected, our willingness to trust the Lord to help us forgive our abusers and failed protectors will determine whether or not we experience the healing we seek. Though we cannot fully forgive without experiencing healing, we cannot experience complete healing without being willing to forgive. We cannot have one without the other.

Forgiveness means letting go of the judgments we've formed about what others deserve because of their actions. Holding on to those judgments will cause us to lose sight of the truth of God's love and mercy toward His children, ourselves included. We can choose freedom from the judgments we've formed by rejecting them—again and again, as many times as necessary.

When we resist the hard work of walking out forgiveness toward ourselves or others, the root of our resistance is often self-preservation. However, we can learn to trust God to protect our hearts from the lies brought on by our abuse experience.

Lord, help me to forgive my abuser and those who failed to protect me. I want to be free to see myself and others the way You see them, free to experience Your grace and mercy, and free to love others the way You've called me to love them. I pray that You will heal the wounds and speak truth to the lies that lead me to protect my own heart with anger and judgment. I want to trust You to be the protector of my heart. Amen.

What Forgiveness is and What it is Not
By Jeff and Lynné Ray

What forgiveness is NOT:

Forgiveness is not a proclamation of trust. Saying "I forgive you" is not the same as saying, "I trust you."

Forgiveness is not a response to an apology. It is a response to a biblical command. The process of forgiveness begins and ends within my own heart. I can choose to forgive someone long before they ever confess to any wrongdoing or apologize for it.

Forgiveness is not saying that "what you did was okay." Romans 6:1-2 says, "What shall we say, then? Shall we go on sinning so that grace may increase? By no means! We are those who have died to sin: how can we live in it any longer?" A relationship with someone who takes advantage of your forgiveness, may need to be reevaluated. Our forgiveness needs to be sincere, but we need to be strong enough to put up proper boundaries as well.

Forgiveness is not instantaneous. It is a process that continues until we are willing to honestly deal with the hurt and the pain we feel.

Forgiveness is not a sign of weakness. The ability to sincerely forgive someone is actually an act that takes an incredible amount of strength and character, so much so that it is something we aren't fully capable of in our own strength. We must seek the Lord for the strength and healing to forgive.

What forgiveness IS:

Forgiveness is a command: We don't forgive because we feel like it; we forgive because we are commanded to. We forgive because the Father forgives us (Matt 6:14-15). Unforgiveness impacts our prayers (Matt 11:25) and our marriages (1 Peter 3:7). An unwillingness to forgive, to meet someone where they are, to view others with compassion and love, actually affects and hinders our own spiritual growth. If we want to be our best, and receive God's best, then we must choose to forgive.

Forgiveness is a choice. It is a choice that sometimes has to be made day by day, minute by minute, but it is a choice, nonetheless. It makes it really hard to be a forgiving person when I allow myself to continually dwell on what the other person has done. As time goes on, those thoughts could begin to diminish, but not if we continue to choose to hang on to them. If we're not careful, it can almost become habitual, a place we allow ourselves to go when we want to feel better about the hurt and resentment we are choosing to cling to. When those reminders come up, and they will, we need to knock them down with the truth. God is bigger than any betrayal. He can give us the strength we need every day to let go of the past and move forward the future.

> _"Therefore, as God's chosen people,_
> _holy and dearly loved,_
> _clothe yourselves with compassion,_
> _kindness, humility, gentleness and patience._
> _Bear with each other and forgive_
> _whatever grievances you may_
> _have against one another._
> _Forgive as the Lord forgave you._
> _And over all these virtues put on love,_
> _which binds them all together in perfect unity."_

Colossians 3:12-14

Chapter 10 Discussion

1. Can you identify judgments you've made about what your abuser deserves? What are they?

_____

_____

_____

_____

_____

_____

_____

2. Write a prayer renouncing your judgments.

_____

_____

_____

_____

_____

3. Write out Isaiah 40:31 in your favorite translation. What part stands out to you the most from this verse? Write out your thoughts or a prayer.

_____

_____

_____

_____

_____

_____

4. Do you resist forgiving your abusers and/or failed protectors? Do you trust the Lord to protect your heart if you let go of your anger? Write out your thoughts.

_____

_____

_____

_____

_____

_____

5. Write out a prayer asking the Lord to help you trust Him to be your protector.

_____

_____

_____

_____

_____

_____

6. If you are ready, write out a prayer of forgiveness for your abuser. If you're not ready to do that, confess your feelings to the Lord and invite Him to continue healing your heart.

_____

_____

_____

_____

_____

_____

7. The author's story of forgiving herself for her perceived role in her father's death is unique in many ways, but it is not the only way to feel guilt or otherwise take

on the responsibility for someone else's actions. Is this something you've struggled with? If yes, explain.

_____

_____

_____

_____

_____

_____

8. Write out a prayer of forgiveness toward yourself for any grudge or anger you've held about the way you responded to any part of your abuse experience. If necessary, write, "I release myself from _____."

_____

_____

_____

_____

_____

_____

9. What other thoughts do you have about this chapter? What else is the Holy Spirit saying to you?

_____

_____

_____

_____

_____

_____

_____

_____

Chapter 11: Onward to Good Things

I can still vividly remember the exact moment I realized my heart was completely healed from the wounds caused by being sexually abused: a Saturday evening, the third weekend in September 2013. It was my first Encounter Retreat in about two years, and one that represented a lot of firsts for me; it was the first retreat I'd attended since writing my whole story and sharing it with Lynné, as well as the first retreat I'd attended in nearly ten years as a participant rather than as a leader. We were in a session that specifically deals with traumas and sins that were committed against us, and, also for the first time, the leading pastor was speaking specifically about sexual abuse. He asked everyone who had experienced sexual abuse to stand for a time of personal ministry. [Side note: I realize for those not familiar with Encounters that this probably sounds insensitive and terrifying, but in that context it's truly not.] So, I stood.

And I waited.

Waited for something to rise in my heart—fear, shame, discouragement, *something*. But there was nothing there. I thought back over the previous two years—years I'd spent grieving the loss of my best friend, being a full-time college student, and homeschooling my two middle-schoolers—and tried to recall a trigger of any kind, or even the smallest instance of continued sexual dysfunction, but there was none.

I can't describe the wonder that flooded my heart right then, not only because I was healed, but because I had been healed for two years and hadn't even known it. *How could I not know?* I'm still not sure, except that life has a way of going on, and we have a way of noticing things when they're there, without noticing when they're not. I know this, though: if you had asked me before that moment if I believed it was possible to be completely healed of all the wounds of sexual abuse, I would have said no. Like most, I believed a sexual abuse survivor could only hope for being *better*—fewer triggers, less sexual dysfunction, a better ability to cope.

But fully healed? With no triggers, no painful emotions attached to the memories, and no sexual dysfunction? No shame, discouragement, or fear?

Impossible.

Yet, there I stood.

As the realization flooded over me, I felt compelled to lay hands on some of the other brave women who stood and pray something I'd never prayed before—hope for complete healing, a desire to leave possible behind and pursue the *im*possible, the improbable, and the-never-before-experienced. Now that prayer has become my mission in life: to inspire hope in sexual abuse survivors who out of desperation just want to be *better*, as well as in those who have gotten better but out of fear or plain old relief, have settled there. I want to see women embrace the hope we have in Christ to experience God's will for our hearts here on earth just as it is in Heaven.

His will is wholeness. Restoration. Healing. Not partial healing, where we're still tormented, but less so. And not someday, when we've left this earth and arrived at our heavenly home.

His will is wholeness, restoration, and healing *now*. Today.

As we've said a hundred times by now, however, healing from the wounds of sexual abuse is a journey. It takes time and space and courage and pertinacity to complete. One recovery workbook is unlikely to get you to the end, but hopefully what you've learned through these 11 eleven chapters is that the end exists, and you will get there. You *can* pursue healing. You *can* position your heart to receive it. You can trust the Lord's heart is turned toward you; He is for you; He is willing and able to complete the good work He began in you[29].

---

[29] Philippians 1:6

Your part in the process will continue to be just as it was in the beginning: ask and keep asking, seek and keep seeking, knock and keep knocking[30].

Continue to position your heart to receive healing rather than to cope with your wounds. Continue to pour your heart out like water in the presence of the Lord. Continue to renew your mind, reject false judgments, feel your feelings, confess your fears and invite the Lord into your heart's reality. Continue to listen to your thoughts and entrust your worries to Him as often as necessary. Continue to rest.

And one more thing. When the day comes that you realize you've been completely healed of the wounds your sexual abuse experience caused, don't stop there.

Continue positioning your heart for healing.

Continue pursuing all the freedom, all the healing, all the deepest-heart security the Lord has for you. Continue seeking His heart in all things and continue to see Him move mountain after mountain you didn't think could be moved.

The wounds from your sexual abuse experience are but one layer of brokenness—perhaps the deepest layer, but still just one. You have a lifetime of greater healing, greater wholeness, greater freedom to look forward to. As the Apostle Paul exhorts us in 2 Corinthians 13:11,

> *Finally, brothers and sisters, rejoice!*
> *Strive for full restoration,*
> *encourage one another,*
> *be of one mind, live in peace.*
> *And the God of peace and rest will be with you.*

Continue your journey, wherever it takes you, and remember the promise: the Lord your God will be with you wherever you go.

---

[30] Matthew 7:7-8

Chapter 11 Discussion

Congratulations! You've completed the *Sexual Abuse Recovery by His Spirit* workbook. Your final task is to take some time to reflect on everything the Lord has done in your heart and life as you've worked through this material. What are you most thankful for? If you've been attending a HOPE FOR HER recovery group, what was the most impactful part of that experience? Write out your thoughts, as well as a prayer thanking the Lord for all He has done and inviting Him to continue leading you in your healing journey.

_____

_____

_____

_____

_____

_____

_____

_____

_____

_____

_____

_____

_____

_____

_____

_____

_____

CPSIA information can be obtained
at www.ICGtesting.com
Printed in the USA
LVHW100603250820
664146LV00014B/2170